By Invitation Only

How the Media Limit Political Debate

David Croteau

and

William Hoynes

Common Courage   Monroe, Maine

Library of Congress Cataloguing-in-Publication Data
Croteau, David.
By invitation only : how the media limit political debate / David
Croteau and William Hoynes.
p. cm.
Includes Index
ISBN 1-56751-045-0 — ISBN 1-56751-044-2 (pbk.)
1. Mass media—Political aspects—United States. 2. Television and
politics—United States. 3. United States—Politics and government—1989-1993. I. Hoynes, William. II. Title.
P95.82.U6C76   1994
302.23'0973—dc20   94-29580
cip

Common Courage Press
Box 702
Monroe, ME 04951

207-525-0900 fax: 207-525-3068

First Printing

For Cecelia Kirkman   —D.C.

For my grandmother, Inez M. Kass   —W.H.

On the cover:

1. Ted Koppel
2. George Bush
3. Louis Rukeyser
4. Bill Clinton
5. David Gergen
6. Henry Kissinger
7. John McLaughlin
8. Robert MacNeil
9. Jim Lehrer

Contents

Introduction

Turn on your television and their faces flicker on the screen: politicians, pundits, professors, and spokespersons for power. Usually male, usually white, usually clad in the dark-suited uniform of those who walk the corridors of power, they exude influence, prestige, authority, and expertise. Sometimes they appear on public affairs programs like *Nightline* and the *MacNeil/Lehrer NewsHour* because they "make news." But more often, they are asked to analyze, explain, and comment on current events. And they appear by invitation only.

The invitations come from those in the news media who decide that—for one reason or another—an invited guest has something to contribute to the program. The people who are invited to such programs overwhelmingly are those who wield power in our society. Rarely do "average" citizens or community activists make it onto this elite guest list. Television's political debates, then, are not between those at the center of power and those challenging that power, or between a diverse array of perspectives competing to define the social and political landscape. Instead, these "debates" feature a narrow spectrum of people who share similar social locations and political interests. As viewers, we rarely hear from those left out of this cozy consensus.

Television is a fleeting medium but it can leave lasting and cumulative impressions on viewers. More Americans turn to television to learn about their world than to newspapers, radio, or magazines. Television occupies a central place in American culture, serving as the dominant source of both entertainment and information for many households.

Politicians perceive the importance of television to both their policy making goals and their individual political careers. Since so much of the political world is created expressly for television, it is increasingly difficult to separate the world of politics from the world of television. Corporate America also understands the importance of television; advertising on network TV is still the most effective national sales strategy for major manufacturers. Citizen activists have long understood the role of television in the shaping of cultural and political life. This understanding has generated debates among activists about how best to respond to the power of the small screen. Given the widespread interest in the place of television in American society, it should be no surprise that television criticism has become a growing field in the 1990's. Despite this growth, there has been an absence of serious analysis of the content of public affairs television.

This book helps fill this void by examining the often-neglected world of television public affairs programs. It brings together for the first time several studies of such programs that were conducted over a five-year period. The studies were first released individually and, while we have refined some of the language of the earlier work, we have refrained from tampering significantly with their original format. In particular, we have not eliminated recurring points in each work because they help to highlight the characteristics shared by different programs, dealing with varied topics, over a number of years. In fact, it is precisely these recurring features which are of most interest to us, because their reappearance in various settings indicates their centrality to contemporary American media.

Each of the studies in this volume was originally released by the national media watch group FAIR (Fairness & Accuracy In Reporting) and each of the three studies was excerpted in FAIR's publication *Extra!*.[1] "Are You on the *Nightline* Guest List," released in February, 1989, was the first of the three studies. We set out to explore the range of debate featured on this widely-acclaimed program by determining who appeared in *Nightline* discussions.[2] The task, then, was to develop a method for systematically analyzing the make-up of this guest list in a way that would shed light on the question of *Nightline's* level of inclusiveness. While it was tempting to focus on the ideology of individual guests—on some kind of left, center, right scale—it quickly became apparent that such a project was unworkable;

measuring political ideology in the abstract is neither helpful nor reliable. Moreover, it would reflect as much about our own political preferences as those of the guests we were trying to study.

Instead of examining the ideology of guests, then, we focused on the characteristics of the guests—race, sex, nationality, occupation—and the conditions of their appearance on the program—whether or not they appeared alone, when in the program they appeared, how much they spoke during their appearance, and the subject matter of the program. This provided us with an overall picture of the *types* of people that *Nightline* features and, conversely, the types that are underrepresented or excluded. Additionally, since our study covered a period of more than three years, we had the opportunity to observe the specific individuals who appeared repeatedly, which ultimately proved to be among the most interesting and widely-quoted findings in the study. We were interested, however, in more than the individuals and types of people that populate the guest list. We wanted to examine more specific political questions about the ideological nature of *Nightline* debates. As a result, we conducted qualitative case studies of several salient issues of the period, exploring in-depth the way the program treated such politically charged issues as terrorism and Central America.

Shortly after the *Nightline* study was released, we used a similar method—analysis of the guest list along with in-depth case studies—to compare *Nightline* with the *MacNeil/Lehrer NewsHour*. The resulting report, "All the Usual Suspects," was released in May, 1990. With this study we had two principal objectives. First, we wanted to ascertain whether there were any substantial differences between what are widely considered to be the best public affairs programs on network and public television. In essence, we explored the extent to which public television provided a diverse alternative to the networks. Second, we wanted to see if the types of people on *Nightline*'s guest list had changed after the release of the original *Nightline* study.

In the summer of 1992, at a time when public television

3

was under attack from conservatives, we worked with our colleague Kevin M. Carragee in taking a closer look at the nature of public television programming. Our resulting study, released in August 1993, was titled "Public Television 'Prime Time': Public Affairs Programming, Political Diversity, and the Conservative Critique of Public Television."[3] The first part of our original report, which is not reproduced here, revealed that the volume of public affairs programming varied considerably from city to city but on average it took up about one-third of the air-time during the peak viewing hours of 6 p.m. to midnight. We made use of a slightly modified method to explore the guests and sources featured on these public affairs programs, moving beyond the news/interview programs to include documentaries, business programs, and weekly talk shows. Given the variety of program formats contained in this study, our analysis included all those who appeared on camera, whether in "live" debates or taped reports. As in the two prior cases, we analyzed the broad guest and source patterns and conducted case studies of prominent topical issues.

When originally released each of the reports included here received substantial national media coverage. Often, however, such coverage condensed our findings into brief statistics that ignored our more subtle arguments and paid little attention to the implications of the patterns we had observed. The more complete versions of these works contained in this volume will provide more substance and context than is possible in a newspaper's wire service account or a brief radio interview spot.

This book combines these three reports with three new chapters. Chapter 1 provides some background regarding our understanding of the news media and their potential function in a democratic society. Chapter 2 presents an overview of, and elaborates upon, common themes that emerge from the three studies, which follow in Chapters 3, 4, and 5. Finally, Chapter 6 reviews the response these studies generated and explores some of the implications of these works for those interested in expanding the narrow boundaries of television's political debates. Issues related to such "media activism" include difficulties and pitfalls for activists in gaining access to mainstream media, and the role of "alternative" media.

Like all authors, we have benefitted from the comments, ideas, and critiques of many people in writing the original studies included in this volume and in producing the new material. The Boston College Media Research and Action Project (MRAP) served as a useful forum for the early development of this work and provided the foundation for our collective research and writing projects. We are indebted, in particular, to Bill Gamson, Charlotte Ryan, Sharon Kurtz, and David Stuart for the many years of support they provided as part of MRAP. Thanks are also due to Matthew Goodman and Marilyn Kennepohl for their research assistance at various stages of the project and to Kevin M. Carragee for his contribution, as a co-author, to the PBS study.

We extend our appreciation to those who provided financial support for the various studies collected in this book. The *Nightline* study was supported by grants from the J. Roderick MacArthur Foundation and the Fund for Investigative Journalism. The *MacNeil/Lehrer* study was supported by a grant from Sallie Bingham. And the John D. and Catherine T. MacArthur Foundation provided support for the study of PBS. Thanks also to Pia Gallegos and the Institute for Social Justice for serving as the fiscal sponsor for the *MacNeil/Lehrer* and PBS studies.

We owe a special thanks to the staff of FAIR for their assistance with various aspects of the studies collected here, including assistance with fundraising, exceptional work publicizing the studies, and publication of excerpts in their journal *Extra!*. Thanks, also, to Greg Bates and Flic Shooter of Common Courage Press for their interest in and support of this project.

Finally, and most importantly, thanks to Deirdre Burns and Cecelia Kirkman for their comments, aid, and patience.

1
Making Sense
of Media Politics

President Bill Clinton "glared" at *Rolling Stone* writer William Greider. The interviewer had asked a question implying that Clinton had a reputation of not fighting hard for what he believes. Clinton's "face reddened, and his voice rose to a furious pitch as he delivered a scalding rebuke," according to Greider's account. "'I have fought more damn battles here for more things than any president in 20 years...and not gotten one damn bit of credit from the knee-jerk liberal press, and I am sick and tired of it, and you can put that in the damn article.'"[1]

The first democratic president in 12 years was being persecuted by a "knee-jerk *liberal* press"? The argument made little sense, especially since Clinton acknowledged that press criticisms of his administration had greatly benefitted *conservatives*, not liberals. Clinton argued that media criticisms were a key reason "the know-nothings and the do-nothings and the negative people and the right-wingers always win." Earlier in the interview he had observed that "whoever does *Time*'s covers is obviously not a fan of the administration...." He had argued that "the press and the Republicans decided that I'd be the first president, at least in modern history, with no honeymoon at all...." He had noted that many Americans had a distorted view of tax changes because "the Republicans had screamed that taxes were going up, and that had been dutifully reported" by the media.

But oddly, when it came time to lay blame, Clinton concluded that he was sick and tired of the "knee-jerk *liberal* press;" the press that supposedly attacked the Democratic administration, helped the "right-wingers," and was in bed with the Republicans. The preposterous nature of the argument seemed not to have occured to Clinton.

Such references to the "liberal press" may seem absurd, but

the argument has a long and highly visible history. At least as far back as the Nixon Administration, when Vice President Agnew served as the administration's point man in an ongoing campaign against the "liberal media," the conventional wisdom has been that the American news media occupy a spot on the left side of the political spectrum. These charges have been so often repeated over the past twenty-five years that they have attained the status of a "fact" that "everybody knows"—no longer requiring verification or discussion. Even when the media themselves address the issue, they usually accept the basic premise that news and public affairs programs tend to reflect a liberal worldview. Debates in the media usually pit conservative critics charging a liberal "bias" against journalists defending their objectivity. For example, media coverage of the 1992 debate about the politics of public television was limited to conservative critics and public television representatives. *Nightline* broadcast a debate between columnist George Will and PBS's Bill Moyers, preceded by a framing report that included comments from three other critics of PBS, all from the right. Front page coverage in the *New York Times* was similar, citing the criticisms of various conservative activists and the responses of PBS executives, but ignoring any other critical views.[2] Such discussions—even when journalists assert their own neutrality—rarely question the underlying assumptions behind the broader argument that American journalism is fundamentally "liberal." As a result, conservative media criticism has become a growth industry since the early 1970's, with the supposedly "liberal" media appearing as a regular, and increasingly easy, target.

The fact that the media's "liberal bias" has almost come to be taken-for-granted has meant that conservative critics have not had to present much, if any, evidence for their claims. When conservative critics do offer evidence to bolster their arguments, it is almost entirely anecdotal, highly selective and misleading, or it focuses on the political beliefs of individual journalists.[3] In any case, the so-called evidence might make for pithy soundbites on the talk show circuit or flashy direct-mail fundraising appeals, but it tells us little about the politics of the contemporary news media. The "liberal bias" charge is misleading and fundamentally problematic.

We challenge the conventional wisdom of "liberal bias" in two ways. First, our analyses reveal that the public affairs programs widely acknowledged to be the best and most prestigious in the United States generally present the world and worldview of those who wield power, defining a narrow consensus about the limits of acceptable political debate. This is a far cry from the popular image of a left-leaning media. Our findings are presented in chapters 3, 4, and 5 of this book.

Second, as we explore in the last section of this chapter, we challenge the usefulness of discussing media in terms of "bias." We are not rejecting the "liberal bias" claim merely to replace it with a mirror-image charge of "conservative bias." Instead, we are calling for a different standard against which to measure and evaluate the politics of public affairs programming. Before exploring the concept of "bias," it is important to consider the broader political stakes in the debate about media by examining the role of a "free press."

Democracy and a "Free Press"

A "free press" is important for a democratic society because citizens cannot act in accordance with their own individual and collective interests unless they are well-informed. The democratic postulate is that citizens have the right to hear the various sides of an issue and express their own preference, whether through voting, lobbying elected officials, or more direct citizen action.

Perhaps there was a time when direct debate and discussion of local issues in community forums and town meetings served as the foundation of democratic discourse—at least for those privileged interests who usually had access to such forums. Today, though, local issues are usually connected to state and federal policies, which, in turn, are increasingly geared to meet the demands of a competitive international climate. Understanding the forces affecting citizens means understanding regional, national, and even global issues. Citizens are generally

9

in no position to directly experience events that may be affecting their lives but which are happening in distant centers of power. The mediating institutions in our society—such as political parties and labor unions—which once served as sources of information for citizens have been crippled by change. Consequently, in a large and complex society such as ours, citizens primarily rely on the mass media to learn about and participate in the public discussion of policy issues. The media, then, have an important contribution to make toward the construction of a more vibrant democracy.

The Functions of a Free Press

Our criticisms of the contemporary American news media are rooted in our belief that news has the capability of contributing to democratic processes. In essence, we take seriously the potential of a truly free press—free from both government control and the forces of the economic market—to serve as a means of communication, a provider of information, and a forum for political dialogue. But how do we know that a press is truly free? What functions should the media be carrying out in order to meet the needs of a democratic society? Addressing such critical questions will allow us to identify the shortcomings of our current media system and assess the future possibility of creating news media that are genuinely free.

There are several important reasons why freedom of the press is an essential element of a democratic system. A free press can serve as: (1) a watchdog against abuse by those in positions of power, (2) a source of substantial information for citizens about social and political issues, and (3) a forum in which diverse opinions can be communicated to others. Each of these functions, which overlap and are inter-connected, deserves closer consideration.

1. Media as Watchdog

J.S. Mill argued in "On Liberty" that "The time, it is to be hoped, is gone by when any defense would be necessary of the 'liberty of the press' *as one of the securities against corrupt or tyrannical government*" (emphasis added).[4] When the media guard against potential abuses of government and those in other positions of power we say they are serving their role as "watchdog."

The watchdog metaphor is a telling one. Watchdogs serve their owners by alerting them to intruders who threaten life and property. Their bark is intended to summon their owners to defensive action. Similarly, since citizens cannot devote their constant attention to the machinations of politics, a free press has traditionally served as a watchdog to call the public's attention to the misdeeds and threats of those in power. With an increasingly complex (and often highly secretive) government bureaucracy, it is especially important for journalists to serve, in some sense, as representatives of the public in uncovering and publicizing official misdeeds, and thereby providing citizens with the information they need to act.

But times have changed. While the media's watchdog role may once have been taken for granted, that is no longer the case. Jeff Gralnick, former-executive producer of one of the nation's highest-rated news programs, ABC's *World News Tonight*, has argued that "It's my job to take the news as [government officials] choose to give it to us…. The evening newscast is not supposed to be the watchdog on the government."[5] Such bluntly honest admissions suggest that the media have strayed far from their role as a watchdog. Most citizens would not be comforted to learn that some in the media think their responsibility is to pass on news as defined by the government. This used to be the definition of propaganda, now it passes for journalism.

While the reality of a watchdog media is certainly in question, the popular image of the aggressive investigative reporter is still a powerful one. This image is commonly personified by Watergate reporters Robert Woodward and Carl Bernstein of *The Washington Post*. The book[6] and especially the film *All The President's Men* made Woodward and Bernstein everyday cultural references that evoke the image of tough, adversarial reporters who are willing to turn over any stone in search of the truth, no matter who tries to stop them. In fact, Watergate is often invoked as the quintessential example of the media playing the role of "watchdog" in relation to the government—exposing greed, corruption, and ineptitude.

The basis for the image is suspect at best. First, most media outlets were reluctant to carry—let alone pursue—the Watergate story, not wanting to get too far ahead of what was "safe" to publish. Whatever investigative gumption Woodward and Bernstein exhibited was not typical of the media, it was the rare exception. Second, during the Watergate period, other more significant stories were *not* aggressively pursued by the press, including the U.S.'s secret bombing of Cambodia and the U.S. role in overthrowing Chile's Allende government.[7] Finally, the lesson many take from the Watergate incident is somehow that the "system worked"—corrupt government officials and their conspiratorial aides were swept from the White House. In fact, everything from the pardoning of Nixon (which paved the way for his subsequent rehabilitation as a "statesman"), to the more significant Iran-Contra scandal, and the continuing role of money in politics, points to the woeful inadequacies of a corrupt political system and a timid press.

But regardless of the inaccuracy of the Woodward and Bernstein myth, it is the lingering image of an aggressive, fearless press that is of importance today. Media criticism from corporations, the White House, and well-funded conservative think-tanks has helped to strengthen the cultural image of an oppositional media. It is no wonder, then, that popular discussions often begin with the assumption that the media play the role of "watchdog," sometimes even too fiercely.

The myth of an aggressive press continues to persist, in part because journalists cultivate the image as a means of legitimizing their enterprise and avowing their independence. But the media's supposedly antagonistic stance towards politicians is based more on image than substance. Increasingly, the adversarial stance is based on "personality journalism," as reporters dig into the details of the personal lives and backgrounds of celebrities and politicians. While this sort of coverage can and often does become hostile, it rarely provides the public with

more than titillating tidbits of information. The sordid entertainment value of personality politics distracts attention from
substantive policy debates.

The case of Bill Clinton is a prime example of how the
media have generally focused on the personal characteristics of a
politician, to the neglect of issues of substance. During the 1992
campaign, much more time and space was devoted to discussing
the relationship between Clinton and Gennifer Flowers, than to
discussing the relationship between Clinton and the corporate
interests that bankrolled his campaign. More Americans knew
that Clinton didn't inhale than were aware that he governed an
anti-union "right-to-work" state with a poor environmental
record. The problem is that personality politics does little to illuminate the real substance of politics: the policies which will have
an impact on people's lives. Whether or not Clinton had affairs,
smoked pot, or eats too many french fries will, in the long run,
have no effect on citizens. His policy record will.

Retired Admiral Bobby Ray Inman, who withdrew his
name from consideration to become President Clinton's
Secretary of Defense in the wake of media criticism, may be right
that public officials need increasingly thicker skin to survive in
Washington. However, this is only half of the story. It is the
same press corps that turns over every stone about the personal
lives and babysitting needs of Cabinet nominees that acquiesced
to military censorship during the Gulf War and maintains routine relationships with an array of powerful sources. While a
national media focused on the rise and fall of personalities may
help sustain the watchdog *image*, there can be little doubt that
personality journalism is a far cry from the substantive core of
the watchdog role.

While personality journalism may sometimes bring the
press in conflict with those in positions of power, journalists are,
in fact, partially dependent upon maintaining good relations
with those in power. That is because former and current government officials often serve as key sources for many stories.[8]
Maintaining relationships with such sources is a high priority
for most journalists who, as is well-known by aspiring reporters,

are only as good as the sources to whom they can gain access. Generally, the most efficient sources are not lone individuals, but representatives of government or other large organizations. They do not provide information as a public service, but in order to serve specific political agendas. Journalists who need regular information from reliable sources may be wary of offending such sources for fear of losing access. At the same time, the standard methods of objective reporting virtually guarantee that authoritative voices, particularly those of the government, will be a routine part of the news—often to the exclusion of less "official voices."[9] It should be no wonder, then, that the everyday practice of journalism would make journalists and their official sources more like partners than adversaries.

Journalists are also generally organized around particular "beats" that put them in frequent contact with government officials. The White House, State Department, Pentagon, State House, City Hall and so on end up being the "home" of journalists assigned to those beats.[10] These are the places where journalists look for news each day, and government agencies are happy to oblige journalists with regular briefings, press conferences, and handouts. Rather than maintain a firm "watchdog" pose in relation to these institutions, reporters are just as likely to develop comfortable working relationships with the people who work in these offices. As a result, there is the tendency for journalists to develop a cozy similarity in worldview with those they cover.

The watchdog metaphor for the media is particularly inappropriate in one other crucial respect. Real watchdogs are owned and controlled by their masters. In a capitalist society, however, we ask the privately-owned media to serve a public function. The results have been less than ideal. The mainstream television news industry is for the most part a for-profit enterprise. Even ostensibly "public" television is increasingly dependent on corporate money in the form of "underwriting." Conflicts between serving a public function and meeting the requirements of the corporate "sponsor" are inevitable. Watchdog functions become more difficult as news departments face budget cuts as part of the corporate parent's emphasis on profitability. Serious investigative journalism is an expensive, labor-intensive effort that can take months to produce a single report. It makes little sense for corporate owners who are interested in the bottom line to invest in such efforts.

Finally, in the specific field of television public affairs there has emerged a revolving door between government officials and news analysts and commentators. It's difficult to see the watchdog element of the media when those in government leave their positions to join media organizations and vice versa. Instead of a vigilant maintenance of distance, we see Reagan official David Gergen leave the White House and become a prominent news analyst on the *MacNeil/Lehrer NewsHour*—only to return to the White House with the Clinton Administration. Similarly, Chief of Staff John Sununu joined the media on *Crossfire* after leaving the Bush White House. And after departing from the Reagan White House, Pat Buchanan became a nationally syndicated columnist and news personality, only to take off his hat as columnist and news analyst to wear that of presidential candidate in 1992, from which he, once again, returned to the media.

Instead of serving as a wary watchdog, then, the media often develop a symbiotic relationship with those in power. This relationship helps set the framework for official manipulation of the media.

The Media "Watchdog" on the Government Leash

Rather than having a free press serving to keep government abuses in check, it has been more common for the media "watchdog" to be on a government leash. For decades government media specialists have practiced "news management" and have, in recent years, almost perfected means of manipulating the news media. This does not require any censorship or direct threats to reporters. On the contrary, the techniques of public relations crafted on Madison Avenue are more than sufficient.

Michael Deaver, media specialist in the Reagan White House, minces few words when he talks of the ability of the White House to produce the top story on the evening news night after night. He says, "I found [television reporters] to be fairly manageable...because we were able to give the nightly news good theater, a good visual every evening and pretty much did their job for them."[11] One of Deaver's central points is that White House public relations specialists can be more farsighted than journalists: "Unlike the journalists, we thought a little bit beyond what the story of the day was going to be. We looked at what it was going to be four, five, six weeks down the road and tried to plan for that." The job of government public relations personnel is made all the more easy by a press that has largely abandoned any commitment to its watchdog role. Former NBC News President Larry Grossman has argued that, while the press should ask questions and act "somewhat independently" of the president, "the job of a president is to set the agenda. The job of the press is to follow the agenda that the leadership sets."[12]

The ability of government public relations campaigns to manage the news continues to breed new strategies for disseminating information and creating images. In the mid-1980's the Reagan Administration created the State Department's Office of Public Diplomacy for Latin America and the Caribbean—a euphemism for an official propaganda campaign.[13] Furthermore, "national security" often hangs over the heads of reporters, who are wary of reporting state secrets that might put people or policies at risk. For example, William M. Baker, a former public information officer for then-CIA Director William Webster publicly revealed that "improved relations between the press and the CIA had helped him to persuade three major newspapers or their reporters to kill, alter, or delay articles concerning CIA operations."[14]

Sometimes, however, government-media relations are not so amicably resolved and the government has resorted to more direct tactics in order to achieve its goals. Such was the case with the 1989 U.S. invasion of Panama. After "acquiescing to demands that it open Panama to coverage" after the invasion, the government made it "all but impossible for journalists to do their jobs," according to one *Boston Globe* reporter.[15] For several days, armed guards prevented reporters from leaving the

U.S. military installation where they had been confined "in many cases without food and in nearly all cases without a place to sleep other than on concrete or linoleum floors." After such treatment, "more than 100 members of the news media opted to take a military flight home, ... many of them without ever filing a story."

The 1991 Persian Gulf war, in which journalists were organized into official, military sanctioned press "pools," was a textbook example of the combination of government news management and journalistic timidity. Whether or not the major media were pleased with the restrictions, they did little to change them. Moreover, the military censorship is only the beginning of how and why the U.S. press acted more as a public relations arm for the U.S. military than as an independent media.[16]

While the networks and major dailies presented a steady stream of stories about the press restrictions, they rarely addressed the more important question of why the U.S. press was serving more as a transmission belt for official positions than as independent investigators dedicated to providing citizens with a wide range of information. By restricting media criticism to discussion of the official censorship, the regular journalistic self-censorship never became an issue.

The most obvious way in which the major media restricted themselves was in the sources they chose to quote. The policy debate at home was, in particular, sharply limited by the choices made by the mainstream media. In the early months of the conflict—between August and December 1990—the media were not as single minded as they were during the war. Yet, the bounds of dissent only stretched as far as the debate inside the Beltway. For example, there was almost no criticism of the Bush Administration's decision to send troops to the Persian Gulf in August. Only when Democrats in Congress and a series of former generals began to question the effectiveness of war in the Gulf did the media begin to raise questions about the Administration's policy. Still, the questions were largely circumscribed by the participants in the Washington policy debate, and focused on the most effective strategy for destroying Saddam Hussein's Iraq. Often right-wing critics of the Administration's policy were brought on the networks to question the wisdom of war, while the growing peace movement was almost entirely ignored.

All of this suggests that the news media act more often as a "lapdog" than a "watchdog"—providing a forum for government officials to present their perspectives and squabble among themselves, rather than a site for open political debate. Journalist Mark Hertsgaard may have captured the relationship between news media and government best with his argument that the media have become little more than "stenographers to power," recording for all of us what those in power think and do. Ultimately, this is not an encouraging sign about either the "freedom" of our media or the health of our political system.

2.   Media as Information Source

Perhaps the most obvious role of media is that of information source. The type of information that can be offered to viewers is virtually endless. Everything from home improvement programs to science documentaries, for example, provide information of some kind. Our interest here, though, is with the realm of social and political issues—the area covered by news and public affairs programs. These programs have the potential for providing a vast amount of information that could help viewers better understand the workings of the political world, providing them with resources to make their own decisions and take appropriate action.

One key reason people read newspapers and watch television public affairs programs is to learn more about what is happening in their communities, the nation, and the world at large. Television is in a unique position to bring substantive discussions of local, national, and international issues directly into people's living rooms. Through public affairs programming, the presentation of a wide range of conferences and lectures, and, increasingly, viewer participation programs, the distance between the private world of the home and the public world of politics can be bridged.[17] Television information can be broad, as with the brief scan of world events found in the evening news. But information can also be provided in more depth. At their best, for example, television documentaries can offer substantial context, analysis, debate, and commentary on a given topic.

Limitations have always existed in the media's ability to provide adequate information for citizens. However, over the past decade the shortcomings of mass media as a source of information have been exacerbated because of increased pressure to be profit-making enterprises. Whereas at one time news divisions of media corporations were somewhat protected from the pressures of the bottom line, the media have increasingly abandoned their civic role as conduits of information and debate in favor of their more profitable role as entertainers. In the contemporary news business, as Doug Underwood puts it, "newsroom organization has been reshaped by newspaper managers whose commitment to the marketing ethic is hardly distinguishable from their vision of what journalism is."[18]

The "packaging" of news in order to make it attractive and entertaining has, in many cases, taken precedence over the content of that news. News media, especially television, have resorted to the marketing techniques employed by commercial advertisers to "sell" their news "product." Popular news anchors are identified through focus group analysis. They are dressed to make them appear warm and trustworthy, instructed to engage in friendly disarming banter with other anchors, and sold to the public as news personalities. An industry of "news doctors" has arisen to consult with stations in helping to raise their ratings through the utilization of more "soft" news, slick sets, "action" cameras, and flashy technologies. As a result, local news broadcasts throughout the United States have taken on a startlingly homogenous look that is intended to sell. These stations often take a sensationalist slant in their news coverage, highlighting the drama of crime and accident victims. The industry even has a slogan summarizing this approach to news: "If it bleeds, it leads."

The media's increasing concern with appearance, drama,

and spectacle has been fed by savvy media consultants in electoral politics whose primary function is the manipulative use of the mass media to convey specific messages to the public. Electoral campaigns and the White House routinely have a "theme" of the day which they feed to the networks and newspapers, packaged with attractive visuals and catchy sound bites. The creation of "pseudo-events"[19]—events which exist solely for the purpose of their being covered in the media—has resulted in news which is often the coverage of the *simulation* of events, complete with prepared camera angles and backdrops, rather than actual events.

Increasing concern with image-making and appearance in the news has been accompanied by a decline in the serious substance which a citizenry requires to make informed decisions in a democracy. The near extinction of network sponsored news documentaries is one good example of this. Moreover, the pressure for increased profitability has resulted in the cutting of news personnel, contributing to a further erosion of the quality of news programming.

The gap between image and substance was never greater than with the Reagan presidency when voters repeatedly expressed disapproval of specific Reagan policies yet continued to approve of the president (the "image" of the president?) overall. Reagan's skillful manipulation of the press and his ability to project favorable images led him to be dubbed the "teflon" president. Serious criticism of his policies didn't seem to stick in light of his skillful use of media imagemaking. The Reagan presidency—presided over by a former Hollywood actor—set the standard for the manipulative use of mass media and their imagemaking capabilities. It represented the triumph of spectacle over substance. The lessons of this period have not been lost on more recent administrations who have continued to use the techniques developed in the Reagan era.[20]

Ultimately, instead of in-depth analysis of an increasingly complicated and interdependent globe, we have photo-opportunities, seven-second sound bites, and a growing commitment to "infotainment."

3. Media as the Forum for Diverse Opinions

In order to be active participants in a democratic society, citizens need information about their world. But if citizens are to be active participants in the democratic process, they need information from a wide range of sources, about a wide range of people and events. They need information regardless of the preferences of those with political or economic power. In short, functioning democracies need a truly free media system, one which is not constrained by state or private interests.

In its role as information source, the media ought not to tell viewers what to think. Instead, news should expose viewers to what others are thinking and doing. The role of the news media should be to present the views of diverse groups involved in or affected by any given issue. If citizens in a democracy are to make informed decisions, they must have access to the range of opinions available on potentially controversial matters. Ideally, people representing different perspectives in this range of opinion should have the opportunity to present their case and perhaps debate those with differing views. Thus, rather than providing a pre-digested view of current events, or one that equates "debate" with the views of the two major political parties, television news can serve as a forum that allows for a broad "exchange of ideas." By providing multiple perspectives on issues and events, television can expose us to the worlds and worldviews of a wide range of people.

Mass media have the capacity for introducing viewers to the experiences and thoughts of people living on the next block, across the nation, or the other side of the world. Indeed, since its inception, television has been lauded for its ability to bridge regional, national, and cultural differences. But if news is to serve democratic purposes and live up to its potential, then a commitment to looking beyond convention, moving outside of insider circles, and including fresh perspectives is essential.

Freedom of the press now needs to be understood as freedom of access to the media for citizens with widely divergent points of view. The mainstream media, though, usually do not see it that way. Thus instead of a free and open media that serve as a forum for diverse opinions, we have news media outlets centralizing into mega-corporate empires offering access only to elite representatives of other powerful institutions.

The Power of Money

There are a number of reasons why the media have moved away from anything that resembles an ideal of a "free press." Analyzing these diverse forces is not our task in this work.[21] However, we should note the special role that economic factors have had in shaping the news media. As we argue above, the increasing pressure to make news for a profit has led television media to change the way they produce news broadcasts. But there are other economic forces at work as well.

Ownership

News media in capitalist societies and in the United States in particular, face two important kinds of economic pressures which have contributed to the erosion of a "free press." First, is the cost of ownership. The technological sophistication of contemporary media has opened doors of potential communication that would have been unimaginable to those who wrote the first amendment to the U.S. Constitution. But at the same time, changing media technology has made citizen access to media more problematic. Neighborhood print shops producing influential political pamphlets have been superseded by more centralized media. While personal computers have made small-scale technology more accessible, most Americans now get their news from national network television and increasingly even "hometown" newspapers are owned by multinational corporations.

Today's reality is that capital needed for any substantial media operation is available only to a few major corporations. According to media critic Ben Bagdikian, as of 1992, only 20 corporations are responsible for over half of the U.S. sales of newspapers, books, magazines, television, and motion pictures.[22] The enormous cost of establishing a major media outlet necessitates the raising of considerable investment capital and has contributed to the concentration of media ownership. In order to compete in the media market any alternative product must also have the financial backing of major corporate resources. This precludes the establishment of media not sanctioned by the mainstream economic community. The "free press," then, is free only to those who have access to the enormous capital needed to support such a venture.

One of the consequences of this economic reality is the growing centralization of media ownership. Individual media enterprises find it more and more difficult to compete with multinational conglomerates that are capable of sustaining ongoing losses in a particular market while eliminating local competition. Media conglomerates are buying out local media organizations and creating national and international chains of media outlets. The most prominent examples of this trend are the Time-Warner merger and the high-stakes bidding between ViaCom and QVC for control of Paramount.

There is no simple equation between the concentration of media ownership and the content of media products. However, it stands to reason that diversity in content is more likely to thrive when there is diversity in ownership and control. In addition, the major multinational corporations that own many media outlets are often involved in a whole range of activities that fall in the realm of public affairs. They produce goods that use up natural resources. They hire workers and are affected by laws regulating wages and working conditions. They often receive government contracts. They are affected by tax and other legislation before Congress. They often have holdings in other countries that could be affected by U.S. foreign policy. It is naive to believe that corporate interest in the news is, therefore, purely educational in nature. On the contrary, the growing corporate interest in media outlets is the result of their increased profitability and their potential political influence—a combination that makes media organizations important strategic resources in the corporate world.

The concentration of media ownership does not just affect news; it also has a profound impact on all media, including the entertainment industry. Centralization of media ownership has been accompanied by horizontal and vertical integration. Corporations own different types of media (book publishing houses, music labels, television stations, radio stations, newspapers, movie studios) as well as enterprises involved in the different phases of media production (paper and printing companies, recording studios, book clubs, movie theatres). Media giants are stretching their tentacles into all phases of production and consumption of media, marketing products—including news—that work together as part of an overall corporate sales strategy.

One of the most glaring examples of the integration of news into broader sales strategies is the appearance of stars from prime-time television programming on local newscasts—following, of course, heavy promotion for the news during prime-time—as part of a report presenting an "inside" look at the hit program. In this case, prime-time programming and news programming work to promote each other. Increasingly, all media products are evaluated in terms of their ability to contribute to broader marketing and sales goals.

Advertising

Another major economic pressure facing the news media is advertising dollars. Media products are not exchanged in anything resembling a traditional "free market" environment. Viewers and readers are not necessarily the bottom line in determining the life or death of a media outlet. Instead, it is advertising revenue, usually from large corporate sponsors, that subsidizes the news industry. The price of a daily newspaper does not cover its expenses; network television news has no subscription cost. It is the advertising revenue that keeps media outlets solvent. Major advertisers, not individual readers or viewers, are the primary "customers" for mass media organizations who essentially "sell" the audience to advertisers.

The media must deliver an audience in order to attract advertising revenue. Television ratings and newspaper circulation figures, therefore, are of some importance. But unlike democratic elections, viewers and readers don't count equally.

That is, advertisers are not interested in just the sheer number of viewers or readers. Instead, they are concerned with attracting an audience with enough disposable income to purchase the products being sold. A smaller but more "upscale" audience can generate more advertising revenue for media outlets than a larger but less affluent one. The importance of the advertising dollar to the survival of the news media, then, tends to create media that are especially sensitive to the desires of the affluent.

Ultimately, the rhetoric of free speech runs up against the powerful economic forces of ownership and advertising. These forces, in effect, limit access to the media. According to former Supreme Court Justice William Brennan:

> Freedom of speech does not exist in the abstract. On the contrary, the right to speak can flourish only if it is allowed to operate in an effective forum—whether it be a public park, a schoolroom, a town meeting hall, a soapbox, or a radio and television frequency. For in the the absence of an effective means of communications, the right to speak would ring hollow indeed. And, in recognition of these principles, we have consistently held that the First Amendment embodies, not only the abstract right to be free from censorship, but also the right of an individual to utilize an appropriate and effective medium for the expression of his views.[23]

However, the vast economic scale of media enterprises has resulted, in effect, in the denial of access to all those who do not meet with the tacit approval of the corporate sector. Individuals who are not part of powerful institutions are excluded from the utilization of the "appropriate and effective" media that have come to dominate our society.

Even public television, which was created precisely to provide television programming that was not so heavily influenced by the preferences of large advertisers, relies to a great extent on corporate underwriting to fund its programming.[24] Perhaps it is no wonder that PBS broadcasts several regular business programs aimed at corporate America and does little to represent or speak to those sectors of society that are less well-off economically. A "free press," which is supposed to allow for diverse expression of opinion, is threatened through its ownership and subsidization by one powerful social strata, the corporate community.

The role of the news in contemporary American society has been widely discussed in the 1980's and 1990's, particularly at times of national elections. But the debates that have dominated discussion of the media have centered, not on the gradual loss of a free press, but, as we have noted, on the supposed "liberal bias" in the media. It is to this argument that we now turn.

The Meaning of Media "Bias"

Most popular discussions about the politics of the news media ultimately make their way to a charge of journalistic "bias." Critics from both the left and right have long used this language in their analyses of news media, focusing their arguments on the biased nature of reporting. Despite their use of common language, critics from different political perspectives, not surprisingly, have significantly different positions on the nature of the bias they observe. More important, in our view, is the fact that critics from different political positions define and measure bias using different yardsticks. There are several unfortunate consequences that result. For example, we suspect that an interested general public hearing of "bias" debates is likely to find these different usages perplexing. If "both sides" are claiming bias, who should they believe?

Perhaps the most significant consequence of the competing arguments about media bias is that news media, at least in the minds of many reporters, are ultimately let off the hook. Journalists have too often concluded from the uproar that they must be doing their jobs correctly, since charges of "bias" emanate from opposing sides. Criticism from both left and right confirms the "balanced" nature of their coverage. Charges of "bias" from both ends of the political spectrum, therefore, often "cancel" each other out, leaving intact journalistic belief that the media need not change.

The essence of the problem is this: when progressives say media "bias" they usually mean something different than when conservatives use the same term. We cannot simply ask the question "Are the media biased?" Instead, we need to clarify what is meant by the term "bias." Our first task, then, is to unpack the assumptions that lie behind claims of media "bias" that emanate from both the left and right. This is a decidedly messy affair that raises difficult questions about the nature of such concepts as "truth," "accuracy," and "objectivity." But it is all the more important to venture into this territory because most critics who make charges of bias do not address such questions directly, making it difficult to evaluate the varied and often contradictory claims.

The Conservative Use of "Bias"

Traditionally, the conservative charge of media "bias" has claimed that media coverage is not an accurate reflection of the true nature of events. From this perspective, the function of the media is metaphorically envisioned as holding up a "mirror" to the world. Media "bias" would be distortion in the media's reflection of events. In other words, if the news is biased it is because journalists have gotten the story wrong, either due to their own ideological commitment or their poor journalistic technique.

Critics on the political right have long made this kind of argument, charging the national news with willfully distorting the truth because of their "liberal" agenda.[25] These groups claim they are monitoring how well the news media are presenting the "objective" truth. In fact, many critics, particularly Accuracy in Media (AIM), appear more interested in the degree to which the news reflects their conservative worldview. When the news deviates from this perspective, charges of bias are used to pressure the news media to conform to the conservative position.

At first glance, the argument that the news media should avoid bias and report the objective truth may seem perfectly reasonable—for journalists themselves often proclaim their commitment to objectivity. However, conservative critics argue bias when media coverage does not adhere to *their own version* of the truth. At worst, measuring bias as deviation from some single truth can be a diversionary tactic, camougflaging more blatant political agendas. At best, such an approach may be well intentioned but rife with problems. The most significant difficulty in equating bias with being wrong, inaccurate, or untrue is that the critics are the final arbiters of what is right, accurate, and true—a sort of "truth police." This is clearly an unacceptable position in a democratic society that recognizes the multiplicity of truth claims and the right of dissent.[26]

Conservative media critics are well known for arguing that various perspectives—specifically those of their political opponents—should not appear in the news media because they are inaccurate and unacceptable. For example, throughout the 1980's right-wing critics pressured journalists to shun "communist" sources. When journalists did provide the perspectives of so-called communists, right-wing media critics were quick to argue that this was evidence of media bias. In a telling example, James Tyson, a long time Accuracy in Media Advisory Board member, argued in his 1981 book, *Target America: The Influence of Communist Propaganda on U.S. Media*, that the networks have "become so powerful in opinion formation that national survival demands some assurance that they will not be free to disseminate the misinformation and distortions that have occurred in recent years." As a "preliminary recommendation for a solution to this problem," Tyson suggests that the federal government appoint "ombudsmen" for each network, to prevent the broadcast of communist propaganda.[27]

More recently, in 1990, the vociferously conservative Committee for Media Integrity (COMINT) waged a campaign to pressure Los Angeles station KCET to drop the program *South Africa Now*, charging that it was propaganda for the African National Congress.[28] Similarly, portrayals of gay and lesbian issues have often been treated by conservatives as biased challenges to sacrosanct traditional family values. For example, conservative activists pressured many local public television stations not to broadcast *Tongues Untied*—a film about the gay, black male experience—with substantial success. Conservative critics, including several U.S. Senators, also argued against the funding, and ultimate production, of *In the Life*, a program about contemporary gay and lesbian issues.

A more recent example occurred in 1993-94, when the Rev. Donald Wildmon's American Family Association led a campaign denouncing the PBS broadcast of *Tales of the City*, a mini-series based on stories about life in San Francisco in the 1970's, because it contained prominent gay characters. Georgia's lieutenant governor urged his state's public television stations not to run the series. A bomb threat was made to the PBS affiliate in Chattanooga, Tennessee leading the station to pre-empt *Tales of the City* an hour before its scheduled air-time. In the wake of this controversy, PBS, as of this writing, has declined to co-finance a sequel—despite the fact that the original series generated the highest ratings for a dramatic series in PBS history.[29]

Conservative claims of bias—or blasphemy, obscenity, or being "anti-family," for that matter—are the first step on a slippery slope that begins with criticism and ends, all too frequently, with calls for silencing. It is not hard to see how this happens; if "biased" programs are "liberal media lies," as a 1993 fundraiser for the conservative satellite channel National Empowerment Television submits, then arguing that such "lies" should be done away with is the logical next step. Ultimately, the language of bias leads these critics to a policy of censorship; those who do not tell the Truth or have the "correct" positions, by definition, have no place in the news media and should be entirely excluded.

Evaluating the Conservative Position

In our view, the conservative conception of "bias" is both intellectually untenable and politically dangerous for two reasons. First, is a belief in "objective truth." The notion that bias is about issues of truth and accuracy effectively obscures larger questions about power, interpretation, and the social construction of reality. Such a perspective not only discourages debate, it prohibits the inclusion of certain perspectives. The second problem concerns the resulting ideological uniformity. The commitment to censoring those voices that are "wrong"—by whatever definition of truth—works to solidify the power of currently dominant views by locking out any challengers to this worldview. Let us take up each of these troubling aspects in more detail.

1. "Objective" Truth and the "Mirror" Metaphor

As noted above, the news has traditionally been seen as a mirror held up to the world. What one finds in the media, according to this perspective, is supposed to be a simple reflection of the real world. Critics charging political "bias" generally build upon this view of media, which has wide cultural currency. Journalists regularly assert that they act as simple mirrors of the world and popular wisdom about the free press is similarly based upon the notion that news media reflect reality. Even when the media are being criticized for dealing with one controversial issue or another, it is often this image of the media reflecting—not defining—reality that is invoked. It is no wonder that so much media criticism is about bias; charges of bias fit with this broader discourse about the news. But despite its widespread use, there are several problems with this approach to understanding the media.

First, it is clear that even a mirror cannot reflect the whole world. It must be facing a particular direction, including some subjects in its frame and excluding others. The space and time constraints of the news media generally preclude a complete discussion of even the most narrow topic, often resulting in the exclusion of some positions and the foregoing of historical context. Thus the image one sees in the media is far from complete. Even if we accept the notion that the media are a "reflection" of society, it inevitably "reflects" only a small part of society. All of this begs the question of what should be included and what can be left out.

Second, the "objects" being "reflected" in the media are not passive. Instead, people with different interests, wielding different amounts of power, and with different relationships to those producing the news, are actively attempting to influence the content of media messages. The resulting images often reflect the relative power of actors in our society, rather than some "objective" reality. The mirror metaphor implicitly sees the media as safely isolated from the political and economic pressures that affect all institutions in society.

News media coverage, in fact, does not reflect some objective reality "out there" in the "real" world. Instead, news is the result of a social process through which media personnel make decisions about what is newsworthy and what is not, about who is important and who is not, about what views are to be included in debates and what views can be dismissed. None of these decisions can be totally objective ones. Instead, rarely-articulated assumptions underlie the approach news media take in making such decisions. In particular, as a result of various journalistic practices and institutional pressures, "newsworthiness" is associated with power and status. News programming is in no way representative of the range of views on a particular topic. Instead, "debates" are constructed out of variations on the same theme— a theme conceived and promoted by those in power. As a result, the views regularly expressed in the major media are disproportionately those of the powerful, elite segments of society.

News, therefore, is not the simple "truth" and should not be evaluated as such. Journalists are confronted by economic, political, and organizational pressures that go a long way toward explaining the construction of news accounts. At the same time, news media are not removed from the events about which they report; they are an integral part of the construction of these stories. It is naive to think that journalists simply sit back and watch events unfold and then record these events without imposing various interpretations—their own, their sources', their editors'—on these events. Thus, if we are to acknowledge the various pressures journalists face in carrying out their work, we should develop an alternative to the language of "bias" that

31

stresses the centrality of interpretative processes in the production of news.

2. The Political Consequences of Ideological Uniformity

The traditional language of bias commits critics of the right to a problematic view of the news media with an oversimplified understanding of "truth" and "reality" that is stripped of more nuanced ambiguities. But the problems with this view are not only analytic; the political consequences of such a position are even more significant. The traditional bias paradigm is ultimately committed to a brand of ideological uniformity that has no use for far-reaching criticism, debate, or dissent.

A type of journalism that reflects this paradigm is one that conforms to positions of the perceived consensus and eschews alternative or challenging interpretations. In such a journalism, there is no room for divergent perspectives, outside of narrow insider debates. Furthermore, such alternative views are to be actively resisted so as not to incur charges of bias or, as the political right is known to charge, "advocacy journalism." The end result, then, is the silencing of those outside of a narrow consensus and a commitment to patrolling the perimeter to prevent the entry of such positions into the news media.

The traditional language of bias and its twin commitments to the "objective truth" and ideological uniformity make this term both analytically flawed and politically problematic. This is particularly true for progressives who are trying to break through the ideological uniformity of so much of American culture and who are wary about the stories that have for so long been identified as the objective truth. Those who oppose censorship of unfamiliar or distasteful perspectives as well as those concerned about the political consequences of accepting dominant ideological constructions as the simple truth should be particularly careful about the assumptions underlying the language of bias. It is to progressive discussions of media "bias" that we now turn.

The Progressive Use of "Bias"

In recent years, progressive media critics have themselves taken up the language of bias, helping in part to redefine it and to remove it from its traditional ideological commitments. In essence, these critics have built upon the familiarity of the term and its widespread usage in popular discussion of the media, but have diverged from its objectivist position on the news media and its commitment to censorship.[30]

Rather than stressing the ability to find the truth, progressives have reintroduced the issues of power and interpretation into their analysis, suggesting that bias is most fundamentally about the absence of "balance." In other words, since defining the absolute truth is problematic, news media should seek to provide various interpretations of issues and events in order to provide people with the information necessary to develop their own analysis of these issues. From this perspective, bias is not about getting the story wrong, as it is for critics of the right; it is about systematically over- or under-representing certain perspectives in news coverage. The challenge, then, from this revised version of the language of bias, is for the news media to avoid the tendency toward ideological uniformity. In fact, from a progressive perspective, ideological uniformity is the prime example of media bias. The yardstick for measuring this kind of bias is the ideological *diversity* presented by news media rather than the simple truth or accuracy of the coverage. As we argue in later chapters, measuring diversity is no easy task. Progressive media critics face an array of complex issues, including the very definition of "diverse," the range of diversity that is necessary, even the development of a language with which to talk about media diversity. One thing is clear: discussions of media diversity have to move far beyond any simple measure of the "liberal" or "conservative" nature of programming. This makes progressive discussions of media "bias" more complex and, therefore, more difficult to evaluate.

Evaluating the Progressive Position

We share the basic premise of this progressive analysis of media bias, insofar as it calls for a variety of voices and perspectives to be heard in the media. But we find the baggage of the term "bias" politically problematic. Our progressive colleagues who frame their media criticism around the concept of media bias rarely make explicit the distinctions between their own use of the language of bias and the more traditional usage. We suspect this is why progressive critics and conservative critics are often seen as making similar censorship demands on the media. Moreover, even the most astute progressive critics who rely on the language of bias at times cannot help but slip back into the language of objectivity, for it is to these questions that the language of bias ultimately leads.

At first glance, there are some advantages to the use of the "bias" language for progressives. Journalists are more accustomed to this language and may be more responsive to arguments using this terminology. Also, the term "bias" will often resonate with fellow activists who are concerned by what they see as the propagandistic nature of much news coverage. Finally, communicating with the general public is easier, particularly in short television appearances, using the already familiar language of bias.

However, given the historical uses of "bias" claims, we argue that progressives committed to democratizing the mass media need to find new ways to talk about the shortcomings of the contemporary news media. The term "bias" simply brings with it too much baggage associated with the conservative use of the term. The equation of liberal and conservative critiques is made easier by their common use of the language of "bias." In turn, it is far easier for journalists and the general public to dismiss progressive "bias" critiques of the media if they are seen as mere left counterparts of conservative critiques.

In our view, the progressive rewriting of the language of bias has been a step in the right direction. But instead of holding onto the term bias, we suggest that the language of diversity become a new model for progressive media analysis. This new language would help move the progressive critique away from the conservative position, not only semantically, but substantively as well. A commitment to media diversity can be understood as antithetical to calls for censorship and uniformity and instead should be seen as a central element of a more robust democracy.

Moving beyond a bias-oriented perspective toward one that focuses on the diversity of media content is easier said than done. It requires letting go of the tendency to focus on the individual reports that are found to be politically troubling. In other words, media criticism that relies on the single-story method—and takes news outlets to task for publishing such reports—is tempting but does little to move us away from the notion that each story should somehow be "correct." A diversity perspective is only interested in the single stories when they are part of a larger ideological pattern; it is precisely these patterns that need to be explored.

It is also important to move beyond a focus on the political preferences of individual journalists, long a strategy of media critics of the right. Research has shown that individual journalists tend to have personal politics that are, indeed, more closely connected to the Democratic than Republican party. But that does not translate into media coverage that is politically liberal. There are several reasons for this. First, journalists work for editors and producers who wield influence over the content of media reports and who tend to be more conservative. Second, journalists, editors, and producers alike are all employed by corporations whose interests generally lie with the maintenance of the status quo, not with those who challenge it. Third, mainstream journalists abide by professional norms and practices that focus the news away from their own political beliefs and toward the world of officialdom. Fourth, on television public affairs programs, it is the invited *guests* who most clearly have the opportunity to present their views and opinions. Regardless of whether we perceive a journalist to be a political friend or foe, they are still constrained by various professional and organizational forces. While it can be useful to track the reportorial strategies of different journalists, a fascination with the political commitments of individual journalists obscures the broader questions about diversity in the news.

It should also be noted that media personnel tend to share the demographic characteristics of those in other positions of power: they are disproportionately white men. This is especially true at the higher levels of management. In 1989, for example, 94 percent of top management positions in U.S. news media were occupied by men. And the top five executives at Capital Cities ABC, Times Mirror, CBS, Knight-Ridder, *The New York Times*, and the Turner Broadcasting System were all men. The boards of directors of these same corporate media outlets were also virtually all male. As for journalists, more than three quarters of network news reports were filed by men; and only 27 percent of front page bylines in ten major newspapers were women's.[31] Furthermore, a 1990 study of the *New York Times* op-ed page found that 87 percent of the 309 opinion pieces by outside contributors during the first half of 1989 (excluding Sundays) were written by men.[32]

Despite changes in the 1980's, employment in news media still substantially underrepresents racial and ethnic minorities. Barbara Reynolds, columnist for *USA Today*, notes that in the top positions at news organizations, where decisions are made, at least 95 percent are white men. And less than 5 percent of reporters at U.S newspapers are African-American.[33] According to a 1993 study by the American Society of Newspaper Editors, a total of 10.25 percent of newsroom professionals at the countries largest 1,535 dailies are minorities. But the vast majority of minority journalists work at big city newspapers; 45 percent of U.S. newspapers still have newsrooms that are entirely white.[34]

Evaluating Media Politics

Our analysis of public affairs programming focuses on sources and guests, not on journalists. In essence, we argue that the best strategy for understanding the politics of the news media is to examine the voices that appear in the news. Since journalists have been trained to keep their explicit interpretations out of stories—unless they are clearly identified as opinion commentators or analysts—these interpretations are provided by sources. At the same time, analyzing sources tells us a great deal about the journalists doing the reporting because it is the journalists who decide which sources to rely upon and, with television news, which ones to put on the air. Ultimately, an exploration of sources—or, in the case of interview/discussion programs, guests—provides us with a clear picture of the range of opinion that is considered legitimate and that which is not worthy of mainstream attention. Answers to these questions are at the heart of any nuanced understanding of the politics of the news media.

In the chapters that follow, we examine the sources and guests on various news and public affairs programs with the specific intent of measuring the diversity of perspectives featured on television news and public affairs programming. A diversity perspective suggests that healthy news media should exhibit a range of perspectives on any given issue, representing various sectors of society and various explicit political positions. One of the threads that connects the three studies in this book is our finding that contemporary television news lacks this sustained diversity. In Chapter 2 we explore this and other themes that run through the book.

2
News, Diversity, and Power

Every four years, on the night of the Presidential election, the three networks provide an entire evening of electoral coverage. For those who sit in front of the television, remote control in hand, the evening is spent flipping between the various stations. What becomes apparent, after only a few minutes, is the remarkable *sameness* of the coverage. Ultimately, it doesn't seem to matter which network you watch; they all follow the same basic conventions. A large map is the focal point of each broadcast, and each state changes colors as it is awarded to one of the candidates. Exit polls, often accompanied by colorful graphics, are presented by journalists and pollsters, who explain public attitudes. Expert commentators, invariably current or former political insiders, appear on each network to interpret the latest results. And reporters stand-by at campaign headquarters, waiting for a chance to talk with senior campaign workers and, ultimately, to broadcast the speeches by winner and loser.

The similarity of election news is most clear at the level of *form*. Each network adopts the same formats, patterns, and even timing as the evening advances toward an often anticlimactic conclusion. This sameness is most obvious on election night, but the reliance on conventional forms is central to almost all television news coverage. This is the reason why network news often seems virtually identical, and why the networks are willing to engage in bidding wars over popular anchors; with such similar news forms, it is the individual anchors who give each network a "distinctive" identity.

Public affairs programs also rely on standard conventions, particularly the (electronic) roundtable discussion, moderated by the host. Anyone who watches news or public affairs programs has experienced the sensation of listening to the same old pundits and politicians espousing the same old platitudes about the issues of the day. Sameness, it appears, extends beyond form to the content of the programming. But can we trust our impressions when it comes to such perceptions? Do these broadcasts really confine themselves to a narrow range of opinion, from a narrow type of "expert?" Answering these questions requires a systematic look at the evidence.

In the following chapters, we examine the range of perspectives broadcast on *Nightline*, the *MacNeil/Lehrer NewsHour*, and the broader schedule of public affairs programs on public television. While each chapter focuses on a different time period, ranging from 1985 to 1992, the chapters make use of two common strategies: 1) analysis of the overall makeup of the guests and/or sources appearing on the programs, and 2) more in-depth case studies of coverage of issues that were particularly salient at the time. While the individual guests and sources change from program to program and the salient issues range from the economy to terrorism to the Los Angeles riots to events in China, there are certain patterns that we observe in each of the programs that we studied.

These recurring themes, in our view, suggest the ways that contemporary American news media observe similar norms and follow similar practices. In other words, since our research explores several programs at several different historical moments, the existence of a set of issues that runs across the different chapters tells us that we have not witnessed some anomaly. On the contrary, such common themes indicate that the patterns we identify are both enduring and widespread, at least at prestigious television public affairs programs like those that we studied. Ultimately, these themes are suggestive of much more than the strengths and weaknesses of particular programs. They tell us a great deal about the very definition within media circles of who and what are the proper subject of news. In this chapter, we provide an overview of the themes that animate the studies that follow.

The Many Meanings of Diversity

As Chapter 1 indicates, we make extensive use of the concept "diversity" as a means of assessing the politics of the contemporary news media. In essence, we argue that an important standard for measuring the quality of news is the range of perspectives the news includes. Of course there are other concerns in assessing the quality of news. The depth of coverage and the presentation of context for stories, for example, are other important measures. But in addition to those considerations, we believe that news which is diverse—in terms of the sources, viewpoints, and authors—is the kind of news that is most likely to serve the information needs of citizens. News featuring diverse views is also less likely to serve as propaganda for those in power. One of the common threads which ties this book together, then, is our argument about the lack of diversity in television news. The subsequent chapters demonstrate *how* the news lacks diversity, *who* and *what* are generally excluded, and what the consequences are for the content of news coverage and American political life more generally.

There can be little doubt that "diversity" has become, in the 1990's, an increasingly prominent and contested term. Progressives organizing against racism, sexism, and homophobia, for example, have focused their arguments on the common agenda of promoting diversity. However, advocates of diversity have been cast by conservative critics as zealots promoting a so-called "politically correct" agenda. These charges have been picked up by the national news media, who now invoke the term "PC" to suggest the apparent rigidity and intolerance of those arguing for increased diversity. As a result, the debate about diversity has moved to center stage in the widening culture wars in the United States in the 1990's.[1]

Despite such widespread use, diversity is a concept that generally receives more lip-service than substantive discussion. Since it has become a shorthand term in the broader contest about the future of American society—describing the political goals of certain progressives and the fears of certain conservatives—there has been little effort to define what diversity means or how and why it is of political relevance in various social arenas. As far as the news media are concerned, the widely publicized rhetoric about achieving diversity has not been matched by any clear analysis of what the relationship between diversity and media is all about.

One level of analysis which is regularly discussed concerns the diversity of media personnel. As noted in the previous chapter, media personnel at the higher levels of authority are disproportionately white males. And while younger journalists and journalism school students have become an increasingly diverse lot, most reporting staffs still dramatically underrepresent woman and minorities. But our analysis is of the media *product*—actual television programming, not the media industry per se. In our view, news media will promote an active public sphere and, therefore, enhance the possibilities for democratic participation if it attends to at least four types of diversity in its media product: demographic diversity, political diversity, national diversity, and topical diversity.

Demographic Diversity: Race, Gender, and Class

One of the simplest and most readily observable types of diversity in television news involves the demographic categories of race, sex, and class. These attributes are important simply because one's position in national and social hierarchies can profoundly shape how one sees the world. Obviously all members of a particular demographic group do not necessarily share the same perspective, but people's position influences what they see of the world, with whom they talk, how others respond to them, and how they perceive their best interests. If media are to contribute to democratic processes, expanding the demographic diversity of those voices that populate news programs is a central task. In particular, news has the potential to provide all of us with perspectives from people with whom we do not have regular face-to-face contact. In a society which is so severely stratified by such cleavages as class, race, and culture, television news has the capability to help break down the demographic barriers between people.

Generally speaking, however, the vision of this country projected in television news is drastically skewed to overemphasize the views of those with political and economic power or high-status credentials, a group of people who are overwhelmingly white and male. It is clear that those in positions of power, especially elected officials, will have regular access to the media and, in turn, should be subjected to media scrutiny. And in contemporary American society, those who hold powerful offices and positions are disproportionately white men. There is no way for the media to avoid this fact. However, in a democratic society, media that report only on powerful elites do a disservice to the public by communicating predominantly one perspective on the world.

If viewers of the news are to understand the context and implications of government and economic policymaking, they need to hear from more than the elite "decision-makers." They should have the opportunity to hear the perspectives of those who are affected by those policies and of those who work with affected segments of the population. If the news is supposed to inform its viewers about the state of the nation and the world, then it needs to find ways to communicate the views of the majority of the population: women, racial and ethnic "minority" groups, and the poor and working classes. If the news is supposed to promote understanding in a democratic society, then it needs to attend to the ultimate *source* of democratic power by reporting on "regular" people and their relationship to—or alienation from—the political process.

We are not arguing that any type of quota system should exist—where the percentage of women, for example, among the experts quoted on the news must equal the percentage of women in the population as a whole. Any strict formula would be absurdly unworkable and undesirable. However, the findings we report in subsequent chapters do indicate the degree to which the news lacks anything resembling appropriate demographic representation. The absences are so striking and the reliance on a demographically narrow range of voices so routine, that it is easy to simply accept the lack of diversity as "natural." We argue that the first steps toward expanding the range of voices on television news is to challenge the assumptions that define news in this narrow fashion and identify those relevant parties who are regularly missing from public affairs coverage.

As we will demonstrate, demographic diversity usually is not achieved. For example, reporting on the economy relies heavily on the pronouncements of government officials, corporate executives, and academic experts. A more diverse approach would include the views of unions and other labor-based organizations, consumer groups, and the views of workers who are most directly affected by economic policy changes. Coverage of national budget priorities often relies on the perspectives of government and corporate officials to the exclusion of representatives of communities of color, women's organizations, recipients or providers of social services, and other "unofficial" perspectives. And discussions of the environment reflect the views of federal and state government officials, regulators, and corporate polluters, but largely exclude representatives from environmental organizations or members of the communities, often in poor, urban neighborhoods, that pay the price for environmental degradation.

Any discussion of the need for increased demographic diversity inevitably confronts two dangers: tokenism and ghettoization. One cynical response to the call for increased diversity is to rely upon a small group of elite sources with appropriate demographic characteristics. So instead of the usual white male elites, programs begin to feature elite women and people of color. It is not surprising to see journalists responding to calls for the news to become more "representative" by trying to address the most visible forms of diversity. It is easy for both journalists and the viewing public to observe diversity in terms of race and sex on television public affairs programs. What is more likely to be overlooked is the homogenous class status of those who are regularly featured.

When debates are populated by elites, regardless of their other demographic characteristics, significant perspectives are excluded. Such a strategy removes the issues of class and power from the table. Lest we forget, not all white men walk the halls of power. White working class and poor men are as rare a commodity on television as women and people of color. Thus, while attending to demographic diversity must include discussion of race and sex, it must also encompasses the issue of class power.

Even when the sources are not insiders, demographic diversity is frequently reduced to finding *one* source, to be featured regularly, to fill an identified whole. Specific individuals, well-intentioned or otherwise, can become token representatives for entire communities, often against their own wishes.

The documentary film "Race Against Prime Time," which explores media coverage of the 1980 riot in Miami, provides a dramatic example of this phenomenon. Marvin Dunn, a professor at Florida International University, became a popular source for both local and national television news, presenting interpretations that were considered by many to be insightful. As an African American, Dunn fit the demographic category that reporters were looking to fill, and he was implicitly identified as a spokesperson for the black community. Even though Dunn became the most widely quoted black source—one of a very small number of blacks to whom the television cameras turned—he was a relatively unknown university professor with little connection to the community in turmoil. Dunn recognized the problems with this kind of reporting, noting: "It is incredible that the community could riot and have the media not be able to draw upon a wide variety of people to help interpret those events. They should not have had to talk to me and one or two others only about what was going on here. I might have been dead wrong; some people insist that I was. But who determines how many people are in the card file at the different television channels? I don't."[2]

A second danger is that women and people of color will only be included in discussions of issues that are perceived to be, for example, "women's" or "black" issues. Women, then, become sources and guests on stories about issues that are defined as "feminine" or those that are perceived to affect women directly. For practical purposes, this means that women will be included in discussions of traditionally "soft" news, because "soft" news is often perceived to be for and about women. At the same time, women will be included in more traditional, "hard" news stories primarily when the story is directly about women, for example coverage of abortion, sexual harassment, or female political candidates.

For racial and ethnic minorities, there are even fewer spaces within which to fit into the narrowly defined news norms. African Americans will be included in stories about urban problems, racism, or Southern Africa, for example, and Latinos will appear in discussions of immigration, bilingual education, or Latin America. Journalist Carolyn Craven has described this phenomenon. "Blacks are called in to discuss issues that either predominantly affect Blacks in this country or that affect Africa. As though we have no opinions on the environment or about China or about Central America or Eastern Europe. I would love to comment on all of those subjects and have informed opinions on all those subjects. Even when we are called in, we're called in to represent such a narrow focus as though Blacks' only concerns are about what other Blacks are doing, either in this country or abroad. And that's *truly* offensive."[3] Ultimately, on issues that do not have an obvious gender or race hook, there is little room for the voices of women and minorities.

The impact of such patterns of inclusion and exclusion should not be underestimated. Too often it appears that women or people of color are "special interests" because they are ghettoized to discussions about "their" issues. When women and minorities are implicitly defined as "special interests" with their own narrowly-defined concerns, they become easier to exclude (or when they are included, they are easier to dismiss) from discussions about issues with which they do not have a direct stake. Meanwhile, white male elites are a disproportionate and pervasive presence in discussions of virtually all issues. This clear differentiation in access patterns suggests in a not-so-subtle manner that the perspectives of the white and male guests represent the opposite of the "special interest;" they implicitly represent the universal interests of the nation.

Ultimately, news coverage needs to be demographically inclusive as a recognition of the multiple perceptions of reality that exist in our society. While demographic diversity will not guarantee that different ideas will always be heard, it is one sign of a healthy debate.

Political Diversity

Demographic diversity can only go so far in ensuring that robust debates will appear on television news. While it is valuable on its own, demographic diversity needs to be supplemented by a conscious effort at substantive political diversity. A commitment to political diversity helps to ensure that not only will we see the perspectives of different types of people, we will also hear a wide range of ideas. It is a means of guaranteeing that viewers will have access to different definitions of problems, different suggestions for solutions, and different depictions of important players in local, national, and international conflicts. Such wide-ranging debates are essential for a healthy democracy, and the national reach of television makes it an opportune medium for providing multiple perspectives of issues and events so that citizens can develop their own views and act accordingly.

The importance of the inclusion of a range of perspectives is tacitly recognized in the media coverage of some issues. For example, coverage of the abortion debate has included the voices of activists on all sides of this issue, medical and legal experts, as well as government officials. This is an example of the kind of diversity that is essential for television news. Journalists seem to have recognized that a wide range of opinions—not just "pro" and "con"—exist on this issue. As a result, not only do official and authoritative voices appear, but voices of women who will be most directly affected by abortion laws are included. Admittedly, reporting has often lacked demographic diversity, focusing disproportionately on white women with professional jobs, to the exclusion of women of color and working class and poor women. Despite such serious shortcomings, reporting on abortion has often presented many different perspectives indicating that political diversity is attainable.

Unfortunately, broad political diversity is rarely achieved in the U.S. news media. Instead the range of political opinion usually emphasized in the media is a tightly constricted one which is centered in Washington D.C.'s elite political community. This leaves out the views of many—sometimes the majority—of citizens. For example, coverage of oil spills highlights the perspectives of federal and state government officials along with corporate officials, while ignoring the views of environmentalists. Coverage of war-peace issues generally includes the range of opinion from Congressional leaders to the White House, but does not include national and local peace and justice groups that do not accept the premise of the Washington-centered "debate." When journalists begin with the assumption that a Republican and Democratic position on an issue constitutes the range of possible views, they are almost certain to be missing an essential component of any discussion.

The inclusion of a more diverse range of political perspectives may seem a difficult task because it entails seeking out unofficial opinions that may be unpopular and unfamiliar to middle-class journalists. However, including a wider range of positions should be, in fact, a rule of good journalism. In a country that prides itself on the right to dissent, the meaning of this right becomes questionable if the television gatekeepers do not allow a broader audience to hear these dissenting opinions. This is precisely what television news generally does: citizens and activists whose perspectives do not fit neatly into the traditional two party debate have little or no visibility. Since this kind of exclusion is so routine and far-reaching, alternative views may not be missed by many viewers who are not familiar with them.

When the issue under discussion evokes strong and immediate opinions, the media's blind spots can seem glaring. During the Gulf War, PBS's *Washington Week in Review* received so much mail about the shortcomings of its coverage that they responded with a form letter acknowledging that the most frequent complaints were "you are not getting the entire story; you are not getting all public views on the war (especially the anti-war view); the Pentagon is using the press as vehicles of U.S. military propaganda."[4] Even when there is no public call for the inclusion of excluded perspectives, citizens still suffer the consequences of a political uniformity that helps repress the emergence of new or different ideas. Despite regular rhetoric on behalf of free and open debate, the national media accept and help to reinforce the definition of "responsible" and "legitimate" opinion by largely ignoring those who would challenge those in well-entrenched positions. The inevitable result is that the political diversity of most major media is severely limited and the same perspectives that lie outside of the tightly drawn boundaries that define "acceptable" opinion are regularly ignored.

National Diversity

Another important form of diversity is national diversity. We live in a world where economic, political, military, and environmental decisions made by other countries can have significant impact on U.S. citizens. Similarly, decisions made by the U.S. government and U.S.-based multinational corporations often have a profound influence on other parts of the world. If viewers of television news are to begin to understand the realities of a shrinking global community, then they need to hear the views and voices of those outside the United States. These voices can be as near as Mexico, where there has been substantial opposition among poorer Mexicans to the North American Free Trade Agreement, and as far as the Middle East, where U.S. policy often plays a role in framing domestic political conflicts.

Even though the networks have increased their international coverage since the 1970's, most reporting is clearly from the U.S. point of view. Since journalists are usually writing for a domestic audience, it is not surprising that developments in other countries are covered in terms of their meaning for U.S. policy or their impact on U.S. citizens. However, the media go further than this in their orientation. In media accounts, even for international events, most sources are from the United States. It is, however, problematic to depict world events almost exclusively through American eyes, for this limits both the range of expression and, equally important, the depth of understanding that American citizens will have of international issues.

A lack of international perspective leaves most viewers and

readers with an ahistorical account of foreign events. This can make developments abroad seem random and spontaneous, rather than the result of long-term social, political, and economic processes. Saddam Hussein's invasion of Kuwait can only be understood as the actions of a "madman" when stripped of the contextual political and economic developments that led up to that censurable event. How are Americans to make up their minds regarding potential U.S. intervention abroad—in Bosnia, Haiti, Somalia, the Persian Gulf, Panama, Grenada, and elsewhere—if they do not hear from the voices in those lands, if they are not given a broad understanding of the politics in those regions, and if they are not aware of the history of U.S. intervention abroad?

The U.S.-orientation of world coverage is so pervasive and routine that the possibility of any broader coverage can be difficult to even contemplate. The taken-for-granted nature of the media assuming an American viewpoint was taken to its logical conclusion during the Persian Gulf War, when the U.S. media used the first-person plural "we" to refer to the war effort, suggesting that all of us—military, media, and viewers—were part of the same team.

As a result, it should not be surprising that Americans often are unaware of the international consequences of actions taken by the U.S. government. A better understanding of the implications of such actions may help shed light on why U.S. policies are often opposed, particularly by developing countries, and why U.S. tourists are not always welcomed warmly. More in-depth coverage of the international role of U.S. corporations may give citizens a better understanding of both the national and global economies. More regular exposure to the concerns and opinions of those abroad may begin to undermine Americans' sometimes ethnocentric and hostile view of foreigners. The regular inclusion of international voices on U.S. news and public affairs program may also help to give U.S. citizens a broader view of the U.S. role in the world, beyond the simple portrayal of the U.S. as the center of the earth.

Less dramatically, but just as important, the exclusion of

foreign voices in media accounts deprives citizens of a potentially valuable source of ideas for addressing U.S. ills. What
might Canadian officials and health care workers prescribe for
the crisis in U.S. health care? What might we learn from
European community activists about reducing drug abuse and
crime? The implicit assumption in the media is that it is the U.S.
who must "solve" other countries' problems. The fact that other
nations may have promising solutions to difficulties which face
the United States is rarely considered.[5]

Topical Diversity

Perhaps the most important role of national news media is its
agenda setting function. The media may not directly influence
what the public thinks, but it can have a profound affect on
what the public thinks about.[6] Coverage of events or issues on
national television news almost inevitably means that those
issues become part of the national agenda. They are discussed
by journalists, policy makers, and viewers alike. The phenomenon of "pack journalism" means that coverage in one prominent media outlet tends to generate more media coverage in
other outlets. Different news outlets often broadcast virtually
identical newscasts, focusing on the same topics night in and
night out.

The impact of such coverage can be dramatic. Take the
example of crime. The FBI reports that violent crime has levelled
off in recent years and has actually declined in many areas.
Meanwhile, the number of crime stories appearing on the network evening news has *tripled* since 1989. This media coverage
has contributed to a considerable increase in public concern
over crime. A May 1993 ABC/Washington Post poll showed that
5 percent of respondents named crime as their most important
issue. One year later, without a significant increase in the crime
rate, that figure had increased to a whopping 30 percent.[7] While
viewers respond to media images of crime, politicians, in turn,
jockey for position in proposing "get tough" crime measures to
respond to citizen concerns.

The issues and events that make it through the media's filtering process and end up on television news are far more likely to become subject to attention or action by both policy makers and citizens than those issues that never become news stories. This is perhaps the central reason why progressive political activists frequently invest resources into media work. They hope that by breaking through the journalistic gatekeepers, their issue will appear on the nation's political radar and there will be a greater chance of changing or introducing new policies or mobilizing new supporters.

It is vital, therefore, that television news have topical diversity among its stories. However, because it must fill a daily "news hole," the media usually turn to sources that have the resources to routinely provide usable stories and information. This routinization of newsgathering can be best seen in the "beat" structure of most media outlets, where journalists are stationed at sites where they anticipate that news will happen. On the local level, for example, assigning reporters to the police station means that you will always have a pool of crime stories to fill up column space or broadcast time. This may be efficient—in terms of time, resources, and dependability—but the practice of going to settings where news will happen leads journalists to define particular kinds of events as news.

There are two segments of society—the government and the corporate sector—that have the resources to support public relations personnel to routinely provide the media with information and story ideas. Relying solely on these traditional sources of information means that the news is decidedly limited, often to the activities of government and corporate officials in major American cities. For viewers, the range of issues available for consideration will be bound by the narrow choices made by television executive producers. Gone will be any sense of alternative agendas as pursued by communities that exist outside of powerful circles. Such constituencies usually do not have the clout or resources to staff slick public relations offices to feed journalists story ideas and to serve as de facto researchers for the news media. Getting stories from places other than well-resourced government and corporate agencies is more difficult and time-consuming for news agencies and, in an industry increasingly feeling the pressure of the bottom-line mentality, it is not often done. As a result, many stories are never heard, many happenings are not certified as legitimate stories, and the news continues to focus its attention on a limited range of players and arenas.

An Insider's Game: Experts, Balance, and Consensus

Absence of diversity has substantial consequences for the way the news depicts the political world. Politics, according to most major news media, is not about broad questions of power—who wields it, in what arenas, under what circumstances, with what consequences—nor is it a forum for wide-ranging debate and controversy about current events. Instead, politics is framed as an insider's debate, where only a privileged few are invited to the table. Journalists are not unaware of the choices they make; they define news in such a way that such narrow debates become inevitable. As Robert MacNeil has put it, in defense of his own program, "We are a news program. When we are mounting a debate, it is at the point of action in the debate. We don't take into consideration on the air, as represented by the guests, all the various points of view that have fed the people who are going to make the decision."[8] In other words, it is the "people who are going to make the decision"—those who walk the halls of power—who are given air time to discuss their positions. Regular citizens should not look to the media as a forum for debating "all the various points of view." That forum, apparently, is reserved for the powerful few. As the following chapters will demonstrate in detail, the result of this view is that public affairs programming features primarily narrow discussions among powerful elites.

The narrow debates that the news media routinely display also reflects an insider *game.* This political game, broadly speaking, is based on the "ups and downs" of political personalities. Such gaming can be seen in both print and television media. *Newsweek*'s "Conventional Wisdom" column features one sentence summaries of events relating to prominent personalities coupled with an up/down/or neutral arrow indicating the fortunes of the individual. *The McLaughlin Group* regularly asks commentators to use a ten-point scale to gauge how much a politician's career is hurt or helped by some event in the news. Sunday morning talk shows often focus on the same questions, in somewhat more subtle form, with verbal equivalents of Siskel and Ebert's "thumbs up" or "thumbs down" for individual political figures. Additionally, regular interest in public opinion polls often focuses on the same underlying question of whether the President has won or lost points with the public after each political scuffle.

Too often in the media, discussion is not about the substance of a policy but the likelihood of it being passed or defeated. Will Congress give the White House a "victory" by passing a bill the president supports? Who will "win"? Who will "lose"? A viewer is often left with the impression that the most important consequence of policy decisions is their impact on the careers of politicians and pundits. This Washington "beltway" mentality trivializes the true significance of policy changes for the citizens and communities impacted by the decision.

It is a political act for the media to ask "who won the week?" That's because, as Jay Rosen notes, a sports-like perspective on political winners and losers, "telescopes our vision downward; it sets a rhythm to politics that permits the media to play timekeeper, umpire, and finally, judge. The question would not occur to an ordinary citizen, but it remains a favorite of pundits and reporters because it appears to place the press on the outside of a process—the shaping of perceptions—that is profoundly affected by what the press itself does. By speaking of politics as a weekly contest of winners and losers, journalists thus avoid any conscious reckoning with their own influence on politics. They avoid, as well, their troublesome need for a more productive political vision, a way of looking at the world that will render it meaningful for others."[9]

What's the Difference Between an Expert and a Partisan?

The "insider" nature of the discussions on public affairs programs means that the same analysts appear repeatedly regardless of the wisdom of their previous commentary or their prior actions when they occupied positions of power. To be—or to have been—an insider, with access to powerful circles, makes one a de facto "expert" on most public affairs programs. Thus a troubling dynamic develops: individuals are qualified to comment and analyze insofar as they are or have been "insiders." The resulting "debates" that are orchestrated, therefore, are often between "insiders" who share a common commitment to traditional politics, to the exclusion of those outside the halls of power.

Expertise associated with insider status also tends to lend sources an air of neutrality. For example, former government officials are often presented as if they are neutral authorities who are invited to speak because of their special brand of "expertise." This belies the fact that they are partisan political actors with allegiances to particular policies and long and sometimes dubious histories in government. In the game of politics, Henry Kissinger is a respected foreign policy guru, not a partisan player and architect of war who now peddles his advice for profit; and Alexander Haig becomes an expert on military issues, no longer a "hawkish" retired general. The same can be said for analysts from privately-funded think-tanks. These commentators often have a distinctly ideological view but are frequently introduced as if they are "neutral" authorities. This neutrality is signaled not only by the regularity with which representatives from such think-tanks appear in the news media, but by the official sounding names of such organizations and "expert" status of their fellows.[10] Those who are considered to be partisan rarely receive such treatment.

On the rare occasions that those from outside of elite circles do appear in the news media, they are clearly labelled as political partisans. Citizen activists or journalists for alternative publications are not afforded the status of "expert;" instead they are identified as representatives of a particular political position. This may be the most appropriate way to identify news sources and commentators, for it provides viewers with a context with which to evaluate political arguments. The problem, though, is that such labels are often applied selectively, and are reserved largely for those who challenge the political status quo.

It is deceptive to represent "insiders" as experts and "outsiders" as political partisans. Too often, though, this is exactly what happens. Ultimately, attachment to what journalists consider mainstream institutions is a badge of neutrality; those who are connected to institutions outside of the traditional mainstream may merit inclusion under specific circumstances, but the assumption is that these outsiders to the game of politics do not really know the rules of insider politics and have a special agenda that they are pursuing. As a result, spokespeople from beyond the boundaries of the consensus are routinely identified in subtle and not-so-subtle ways as individuals who have an axe to grind.

Balance and the Illusion of Debate

The insider nature of many discussions on television also means that apparent disagreements are often less than meet the eye. That is, the range of insiders invited to comment and discuss issues is often so narrow that there are a host of unaddressed assumptions in their approach. For example, debating whether the U.S. should use ground troops or rely solely on air power to drive Iraqi troops from Kuwait leaves unmentioned a variety of assumptions about the desirability of U.S. intervention in the first place. Debating President Clinton's "managed care" approach to health care reform versus Republican attempts to limit reform ignores other possible alternatives such as a single-payer system. The two sides in a television debate, therefore, often agree on more than they disagree.

When insiders who share a general policy orientation meet to debate and discuss the finer points of that policy, the result can often be a compelling illusion of political balance. Rarely does the news ignore the basic convention of providing contrasting perspectives on issues, for this is a fundamental requirement of American journalism. While this standard convention creates interesting televisual drama and protects reporters against charges of taking sides, it does little to provide viewers with anything resembling a wide ranging discussion of events. As a general rule, the two sides reflect the positions taken by the leadership of the two major political parties—even dissenting Party members are frequently ignored. Contrasting perspectives, then, are frequently the differences, generally quite narrow, between establishment insiders. This reportorial strategy does little to inform the public of positions outside of this limited range of opinion; indeed it implicitly denies that other positions should be taken seriously. An alienated electorate that believes all politicians are the same is not far from the truth if one is to judge by the narrow range of views featured on public affairs programs.

On the occasions that these insiders share a good chuckle about their disagreements at the end of the news segment, the game is at least partially unmasked, as it becomes clear that the opposing players are really on the same side when the day is over. Still, the game of politics begins again as soon as the next television camera appears and the players take their regular positions, acting out their roles in a game that costs them little and to which most citizens can only be passive observers.

Even though the debate is framed narrowly, journalists are quick to point out that the news is not one-sided, for how could a two-sided debate produce one-sided news? The problem, of course, is in the drawing of the sides. The studies collected in this book indicate that while the news presents more than one position within elite circles, it neglects the broader public, much to the detriment of a robust democratic discourse. One of the significant consequences of this presentation is a view of the United States without any deep-seated or lasting conflict. On the contrary, domestic conflicts are presented as technical problems that can be solved by competent managers. Political disagreements are depicted as tactical differences, rather than differences in values, goals, or power. And, if they are included at all, those who do not play by the rules of political civility are depicted as extremists who do not understand that Americans are all part of the same team. Ultimately, the depiction of the political world as a game carries with it a clear message about the rules of the game: insider's are the players and only players can win.

As we suggest in chapter 1, the media do not play the sort of aggressive watchdog role that popular myth might imply. Our own work has only limited implications for the watchdog argument. However, one thing is clear: past and present government officials make up a large proportion of sources and guests for public affairs television programming. Representatives of "official" institutions are among the most visible spokespeople on public affairs television and the activities of officials often define the topics that such programs cover.

Government officials are so prominent in the news that it can be hard to conceive of news without them. When government officials appear on the news to defend their policies or to criticize their opponents, seldom do interviewers ask questions that fall outside of the general consensus: perhaps specific policies are questioned but fundamental assumptions are left unchallenged. In short, the news often becomes, in its zeal for official voices, little more than a press agency for U.S. officialdom.

The Absent Public

The chapters ahead also explore the degree to which public affairs programs provide a voice for members of the "general public" in their coverage. We find that, with few exceptions, the public has essentially no role in such programs, except as an audience for them. The question of the public has evolved in our work over the years and it appears most clearly in the study of public television in chapter 5. In retrospect, our inattention to the participation of the public was the result of our own tacit acceptance of the news as a forum for individuals with credentials. Since the public is so routinely and comprehensively ignored by most major news media, except as an aggregate represented by public opinion polls, it can be difficult to conceive of public affairs programs in a broader light. However, it is no ironclad law of journalism that the general public has no role except as viewers and readers.

While we have argued that much of the news can be understood as a set of debates among people who hold powerful positions, we want to broaden the argument to include the importance of credentials in this equation. That is, those with the proper institutional credentials—particularly other journalists, prominent academics, and medical and legal "experts"—can often become regular participants in these discussions. What is significant is who is excluded: those who lack power and the appropriate credentials are generally not worthy of consideration. This is one of the reasons why citizen activists are so regularly excluded; they lack power and often have the "wrong" credentials. Those activists that do find their way into the media often have a set of "appropriate" expert credentials that open up doors for them.

These gates that only swing open for those with power and credentials exclude more than organized citizen activists, although they are quite effective at this task. These gates are closed for members of the public who experience the consequences of the decisions that are debated in the media. Instead of members of various communities providing their interpretations of events and policies, public affairs programs turn to pundits who treat viewers to their insight into what Americans are thinking, often reducing public attitudes to straightforward expressions of frustration, pride, or cynicism. Coverage of the 1992 Democratic National Convention was a textbook case of this process, as pundits took turns explaining how Americans "felt" about the various speeches, remarkably only minutes after their conclusion. When public affairs programs do provide access to members of the general public, either as individuals or in groups, the perspectives are treated as raw materials to be analyzed by experts, who will tell us what Americans really believe, why, and with what political impact. The interpretations that are highlighted, then, are not those of the public, but of the pundits who put it all in perspective.

Chapters 4 and 5 are particularly interested in the degree to which public affairs programs on PBS stations provide a broader view of politics than their commercial counterparts. Underlying these chapters is the question of the meaning of "public" in public television. On one level, we are concerned with the degree to which public television programming provides more access to a public that is largely ignored by most commercial media. On another level, we are interested in the more general patterns of inclusion and exclusion on public television programming as a means of assessing the success of public television in living up to its rhetorical goals of serving the undeserved and providing access for perspectives that do not appear on the networks. While we find that public television does provide certain opportunities, programming by and large fits into the same pattern as other mainstream American journalism. All of this raises serious questions about the public nature of public television in an era of rapid privatization.

Turning to the Evidence

The trends we discuss in this chapter have affected a broad range of news media. But our specific interests lie with television public affairs programming. If the media are *not* performing their job as watchdogs for democracy, if they are *not* providing a forum for the public debate of widely diverse views, whose views *do* they transmit? To answer this question it is important to see who is allowed into the media spotlight—and who is left in the dark.

3
Are You On The *Nightline* Guest List?

On an average week night, five to seven million American households are tuned to ABC News *Nightline*—one of the leading sources of news information in the United States. With its combination of near-universal acclaim from critics and a considerable number of loyal viewers, *Nightline* is an important player in defining the national political terrain.

Despite its widely-heralded prestige, there has been surprisingly little serious analysis of *Nightline*. This study is a small step toward focusing attention on the political role of programs like *Nightline*.

In this study we do not scrutinize the role of the host, Ted Koppel, within the program. Nor is our primary focus on the specific stories which *Nightline* chooses to cover. Instead, our focus is on *Nightline*'s guests—the core of the show's interview/discussion format. To a lesser degree, we also look at the broad issue areas that *Nightline* emphasizes.

Public Affairs Programs and *Nightline*
While there is a large body of literature on the culture and politics of TV news,[1] significantly less has been written about the genre of public affairs television, of which *Nightline* is an example. This genre includes such long-running interview shows as NBC's *Meet the Press* and CBS's *Face the Nation*. The format of public affairs programs is markedly different from that of traditional news programs. Public affairs programs are able to provide news makers, policy makers, and news interpreters with an extended opportunity to interact with reporters and with each other. Like traditional news programs, public affairs television provides "experts" and policy makers with opportunities to reach a significant national audience. However, in public affairs television, these appearances are made within a format which

allows for much more air time than traditional ten or fifteen second sound "bites" embedded within a one or two minute story.

Not only do public affairs programs provide for more interview time and interaction among guests, they also allow for more spontaneity. Since the programs are often live, news editors cannot tightly control what is aired. Guests often have the opportunity to stray from the topic to present different issues and alternative interpretations of events. Thus the choice of guests is crucial to the program's content and character.

Finally, public affairs television is more "intimate" than evening news broadcasts. It allows the audience to see more of a guest's personality. Indeed one of the criticisms of this type of program is that it can transform news from substance to celebrity. Yet, this personal appeal may help to explain why some viewers watch these programs.

ABC News *Nightline* is considered to be the preeminent public affairs program. It undoubtedly has the biggest audience of such shows. With its substantial budget and high-tech prowess, it can provide a forum for debate between guests who are in several different cities, or even in several different countries. *Nightline* also has a higher degree of flexibility than other programs. It often waits until late afternoon to decide what topic to cover; and if a story breaks in the evening, *Nightline* is frequently able to include at least a brief segment on it.

As both an example of public affairs programming and as its own "institution," *Nightline* is an important subject for continuing study.

Overview: Elites, Consensus, and Parallel Agendas

This study is based on all *Nightline* program transcripts for a 40-month period from January 1, 1985 to April 30, 1988. We examined a total of 865 programs, which included 2,498 guests. (Seven shows had no guests.) Based on careful analysis of this large sample of *Nightline* programs, we conclude that *Nightline's* coverage of domestic and foreign affairs suffers from a narrow range of guests and limited scope of issues, which we will discuss under three general headings: elites, domestic consensus, and parallel agendas.

1.   Elites

Nightline's guest list represents a profoundly elite-oriented perspective of both domestic and foreign societies. Overwhelmingly, it is white, male representatives of powerful institutions who interpret the world for *Nightline*'s viewers. Essentially absent from the guest list are representatives of civic and community organizations, popular social movements, and minority communities. Such representatives clearly should be a significant part of *Nightline* debates if these discussions are to include some of the views of people who do not walk the halls of government and corporate power, but who are profoundly affected by the decisions made there.

Instead of adequately including popular representatives, *Nightline*'s guest list is heavily weighted in favor of government spokespeople, assorted "experts," and journalists. Similar imbalances have been noted in other television news coverage.[2] However, this imbalance is even more problematic with respect to *Nightline* since the program does more than just report the news. *Nightline* provides an electronic soapbox from which people interpret events for viewers. Because its guest list is dominated by experts and elites, *Nightline* presents only a narrow perspective of the world, to the exclusion of other viewpoints, and to the detriment of its viewers.

In a very concrete sense, the views of one class, race, and gender dominate *Nightline.* In terms of class, elites and professionals (e.g., lawyers, doctors, academics, journalists, clergy) interpret the world, while working, middle class and poor people and their representatives are provided virtually no opportunity to speak. *Nightline* thereby reinforces the notion that non-elites must play by the rules set by those who have the power to define reality for society as a whole. This is also true in the context of race and gender. Overwhelmingly, white, male, representatives of status quo institutions appear on *Nightline* to interpret events and define situations.

2.   Domestic Consensus

By its limited range of guests and topics, *Nightline* conveys a vision of the domestic political scene that is free of major conflict and devoid of challenging views. If one were to judge from *Nightline*'s coverage, it would appear that a broad domestic political consensus existed in the United States, a consensus which allows for certain policy differences but which is free of deep-rooted conflicts.

For example, of the 865 programs covered by this study, *Nightline* featured only one program about class conflict and only two programs about gender based oppression and conflict. Issues of racial tension were covered a bit more often; however, there were still only eleven shows on this subject in the forty months we studied. While *Nightline* conveys a reassuring image of domestic consensus free of fundamental conflict, the rest of the world is depicted as frighteningly unstable and embroiled in conflict.

To its credit, *Nightline* makes an effort at representing the dissenting views of foreigners. In this regard, *Nightline* is famous for including controversial foreign leaders on its programs. Once again, however, it is usually the leaders—the elites—of foreign countries who are invited to speak. Representatives of popular movements are not usually given the same opportunity. Also, these dissenting views are foreign by definition (and often "anti-American" by implication). This clearly diminishes their applicability to political discourse in the U.S., where the audience is likely to be more receptive to views expressed by U.S. officials pitted against representatives of "enemy" states.

3.   Parallel Agendas

Nightline's reliance on government experts and elites means that the issue areas on which *Nightline* focuses are closely aligned with the U.S. government's view of the world. Issues which were promoted by the Reagan administration became important to *Nightline*, while issues which were inconsequential (or sometimes troublesome) for the administration tended to be ignored by *Nightline*. The worldview developed in the corridors of power becomes reproduced for many Americans via *Nightline*'s circumscribed range of guests and limited scope of interests.

Plainly stated, *Nightline* presents a picture of the world which is startlingly similar to that presented by the U.S. government. *Nightline*'s worldview is one in which terrorism is rampant, with U.S. citizens as targets for no apparent reason; where the United States is under siege from without; where the Third World only exists when there is a crisis or when the U.S. government deems it worthy of attention.

It is a world where elites and experts tell us how to interpret events far and wide; where important events happen primarily to white people, and important analysis comes almost always from white people; where men are both the actors and the interpreters and women for the most part are "ghettoized" and restricted to commentary on social issues.

It is a world where questions are asked about "strategic interests" and international competition; where Vietnam is remembered by Richard Nixon, Henry Kissinger and Alexander Haig, the people who prosecuted the war that ravaged Indochina, not by the victims of the war, nor by those who fought to stop the killing.

In short, *Nightline* evokes a worldview which sees America as "number one"—especially white, male America. It describes a world in which we have to be tough to remain "number one," especially when dealing with the onslaught of terrorism. It is a worldview that might sell well on the campaign trail, along with rhetoric about protecting the family and the flag, but it does not necessarily enhance the credibility of a public affairs program. This worldview, as reflected and promoted by a narrow range of guests, makes *Nightline* fundamentally conservative in the sense of being a program which serves the interests of those who already wield political and economic power in contemporary society.

Nightline's Influence: Legitimation, Limitation, and Certification

Despite all the acclaim, it is not generally acknowledged that *Nightline* and other prominent public affairs programs can have a good deal of influence on political debate in the United States. That is not to say that it plays a direct role in political decision-making. Rather, its significance lies in its role as an intermediary between policy makers and the public. Ted Koppel indirectly acknowledged this in a recent interview in which he said he felt he was qualified, in some respects, to be Secretary of State "because part of the job is to sell American foreign policy, not only to Congress but to the American public."[3]

Nightline helps to "sell" certain political positions by deciding what events to cover and, more importantly, which guests to interview. For each program, decisions are made about what to emphasize, what to play down, and what and whom to exclude. In short, a "framing" process—selecting a perspective from which to view the world—is regularly occurring.[4]

As a result of the exclusion of some political perspectives and the promotion of others, *Nightline* helps to legitimize particular positions. This is especially true of positions which are featured frequently on the program. When the same topic is covered repeatedly over a period of time, with a constant set of political positions on the program, these become legitimate positions. Heard by millions of viewers and quoted on occasion in the next day's newspapers, they become part of the public discourse on current events.

The other side of the framing process is that *Nightline* helps to set limits on public discourse. The range of guests helps to define the limits of legitimate debate and stakes out the limits of dissenting opinion. Most important, the process of exclusion plays a role in delegitimizing positions: voices that are regularly and systematically excluded from *Nightline* seem to have no role in legitimate public discussion. These processes of legitimation and limitation are at the core of why *Nightline* is a politically influential program.

Furthermore, *Nightline* plays an important role in certifying spokespeople. Not only does it legitimize positions in the abstract, but by giving certain individuals regular opportunities to interpret events, "experts" are born. *Nightline* thrives on the concept of expertise. The same experts appear over and over again, ostensibly because of their experience, knowledge, insight or prestige. By receiving this national exposure, they become certified as legitimate spokespeople either for particular positions or for more general issues. Other media will often adopt the spokespeople. *Nightline* certifies and, by interviewing and quoting them, will reinforce their public image as experts.

This process is well known within media circles. As ABC News anchor Peter Jennings has noted, "...television seems to give people an instant set of credentials. Just appearing on the box, whether you're a guest or being quoted, has its own set of sort of electronic credentials, and sometimes they don't match reality...."[5]

Taken together, the processes of legitimation, limitation, and certification make *Nightline* a powerful political and cultural force. The patterns created by these processes are not readily noticeable to the occasional viewer of *Nightline*, or even to one who watches the program regularly. The daily shift from one topic to another and from one set of guests to another helps to obscure the ongoing framing process. A casual viewing of *Nightline* suggests a program with lively discussions that are often fraught with disagreements. Yet, our systematic study of *Nightline* reveals that *Nightline*'s choice of subjects and guests helps to define a narrow political terrain in a way that reflects the interests of the show's elite participants.

Criteria for Analyzing *Nightline*

In selecting topics, preparing background stories, and inviting guests, the *Nightline* staff, like any news staff, must use certain criteria for making decisions about what qualifies for coverage. Since we do not know specifically what these criteria are, we can only analyze the finished product, in this case the transcripts of *Nightline* programs.

In our analysis of *Nightline*'s programming, we also follow certain criteria. In particular, we have adopted some of the ideas put forth by Herbert Gans in his book *Deciding What's News*.[6] His recommendations for "multiperspectival" news coverage include the notion that such programming should be truly "national," which means "moving beyond the current equating of the federal government with the nation." News coverage, according to Gans, should "seek to report comprehensively about more national and nationwide agencies and institutions, including national corporations, unions, and voluntary associations, as well as organized and unorganized interest groups." *Nightline*'s focus on guests from government and corporate circles contrasts markedly with this perspective.

We also adopt Gans' idea that coverage should include a "bottom-up" view in addition to the usual "top-down" approach. Reactions to policy decisions, for example, might be solicited from citizens in various walks of life who would be affected by these policies, as well as from those citizens who organize to change government policies. Again, this differs from *Nightline*'s emphasis on elites and certified experts.

In addition, we agree with Gans that coverage should aim to be more "representative," that is, reflective of the activities and opinions of ordinary citizens from all population sectors and roles (taking into account ethnicity, gender, religion, occupation, etc.). This also is a departure from *Nightline*'s approach.

A commitment to representation and diversity guides this analysis of public affairs programming. This inclusively democratic philosophy informs our *Nightline* study.

Summary Results

Based on an analysis of the 865 *Nightline* programs, we present a summary of our quantitative findings. In the next section, we undertake a more in-depth analysis of seven areas of *Nightline* programming.

PROGRAMS

While the main focus of our study was the guest list of *Nightline*, we also analyzed the programs for broad issue content. During the 40 month period we studied, the issue break-down of *Nightline*'s coverage is indicated in Table 3.1. International issues received, by far, the most coverage; 39 percent of all guests appeared on discussions of international issues, compared to 22 percent for social issues and 19 percent for domestic political issues.

In accordance with these data, much of our analysis will focus on *Nightline*'s international news coverage. These figures also underscore the fact that *Nightline*'s international coverage, and its ability to attract foreign leaders as guests, contribute to the show's prestigious reputation. International coverage is also central to *Nightline*'s role in political agenda setting.

Table 3.1

Nightline Program Topics and Subtopics*
(1/1/85 to 4/30/88)

Topic & Subtopic	No. of guests	Percent	Topic & Subtopic	No. of guests	Percent
International Affairs	**971**	**38.8%**	**Economy**	**208**	**8.3%**
Terrorism/Hostages	165	6.6	Labor	15	0.6
South Africa	88	3.5	Farmers	9	0.4
Philippines	44	1.8	Stock Market	41	1.6
U.S.-Soviet Relations	109	4.4	Airline Industry	14	0.6
U.S.S.R.	67	2.7	Auto Industry	9	0.4
Intelligence/Spying	51	2.0	Trade	9	0.4
Iran-Contra Affair	100	4.0	Other Economy	111	4.4
Central America	68	2.7			
Indochina	8	0.3	**Social Issues**	**546**	**21.8%**
Israel/Palestine	41	1.6	Health	229	9.1
Persian Gulf	44	1.8	Crime	75	3.0
Libya	36	1.4	Education	50	2.0
South Korea	14	0.6	Drugs	26	1.0
Other International	136	5.4	Religion	62	2.5
			Family	42	1.7
Domestic Politics	**466**	**18.6%**	Sexuality	20	0.8
Elections	60	2.4	Other Social Issues	42	1.7
White House	49	2.0			
Courts	77	3.1	**Culture**	**189**	**7.5%**
Military	25	1.0	Sports	100	4.0
Race Relations	23	0.9	Entertainment	59	2.4
Legislation	40	1.6	Other Culture	30	1.2
Immigration	13	0.5			
Homelessness	20	0.8	**Other**	**125**	**5%**
Media and Politics	80	3.2	Disasters	70	2.8
Space Program	24	1.0	Predictions	12	0.5
Other Domestic Politics	55	2.2	Science	8	0.3
			Animals	16	0.6
			Other	19	0.8

* Subtopic totals may vary slightly due to rounding.

Total 2505 100%

Within the category of international issues, 17 percent of the guests appeared on programs about terrorism. Terrorism rivaled the Soviet Union as the most frequent subject addressed by *Nightline*'s international coverage. Nine years after *Nightline*'s birth during the Iran hostage crisis, its preoccupation with terrorism was still evident.

Within its coverage of domestic politics, 17 percent of the guests appeared on the programs about the role of the media in politics. This, along with shows about legal issues (also 17 percent) were the leading domestic issues covered by *Nightline*. Many of the programs on legal themes focused on Supreme Court nominations.

In the realm of the economy, 20 percent of the guests appeared on programs about the stock market. Many of these shows occurred in late 1987, after the stock market crash. Finally, among social issues, health (42 percent) was far and away the leading topic featured. Many of these programs dealt with AIDS.

GUESTS

Ten individuals appeared on *Nightline* more than ten times during the period studied. But five of them (Dr. Timothy Johnson, John McWethy, Sam Donaldson, George Will, Jeff Greenfield) appeared in their capacity as ABC news Correspondents or analysts.[7] The five invited guests who appeared more than ten times were: Alexander Haig (14), Henry Kissinger (14), Elliott Abrams (12), Jerry Falwell (12), and Alejandro Bendana (11). There is an interesting pattern here. The four most frequent guests are either staunch cold warriors or right-wing ideologues, or both.

As has been widely reported in the press, Henry Kissinger is Ted Koppel's foreign policy mentor, notwithstanding the former Secretary of State's pivotal role in the secret bombing of Cambodia and in events leading to the 1973 coup in Chile. Questions about Kissinger's character raised by Seymour Hersh in his book, *The Price of Power*, and other critics have not interfered with his position as *Nightline*'s chief foreign policy expert.[8]

Other foreign policy analysts certified by *Nightline* include hawkish retired General Alexander Haig, and Elliott Abrams, the Assistant Secretary of State who admitted lying to Congress. The one guest on this list with alternative views is a foreigner, Alejandro Bendana, a spokesperson for Nicaragua. Bendana's appearances are in the *Nightline* tradition of having foreign leaders as guests.

Among the U.S. guests, as Table 3.2 shows, 19 people appeared more than five times during the 40 month period, all men. (The most frequent woman guest was Jeane Kirkpatrick, with five appearances.) All but two of the nineteen are white— Jesse Jackson and Harry Edwards being the exceptions. At least 13 of the 19 are political conservatives, most of whom were associated in some capacity with the Reagan administration.

Table 3.2

Nightline Guests
Who Appeared More Than Five Times
(1/1/85 to 4/30/88)

U.S. Guests

Alexander Haig	Former Secretary of State*	14
Henry Kissinger	Former Secretary of State	14
Elliott Abrams	Former Asst. Secretary of State	12
Jerry Falwell	Moral Majority	12
Lawrence Eagleburger	Former Undersecretary of State	10
Jesse Jackson	Former Presidential Candidate	10
Arthur Miller	Harvard Law School	9
William Hyland	Former Dep. National Security Advisor	8
Patrick Buchanan	Former White House Communications Dir.	7
William Cohen	Senator (R-Maine)	7
Arthur Laffer	Economist, Pepperdine University	7
William Safire	*New York Times* Columnist	7
Christopher Dodd	Senator (D-Connecticut)	6
Harry Edwards	Sociologist, University of California	6
Bobby Inman	Former Deputy Director, CIA	6
Noel Koch	Former Assistant Secretary of Defense	6
Michael Ledeen	Former Advisor to Secretary of State Haig	6
Alan Simpson	Senator (R-Wyoming)	6
Marvin Zonis	University of Chicago	6

Foreign Guests

Alejandro Bendana	Nicaraguan Foreign Minister	11
Said Rajie-Khorassani	Iranian Ambassador to the United Nations	8
Benjamin Netanyahu	Israeli Ambassador to the United Nations	7
Ferdinand Marcos	Former President of the Philippines	6

*Titles used here are for identification purposes only.

Tied for fifth place among U.S. guests (ten appearances each) are Lawrence Eagleburger, the one time president of Kissinger Associates, and Jesse Jackson. Jackson's appearances might be attributed to the fact that his presidential campaigns have certified him as a spokesperson of alternative ideas. When *Nightline* needs such a role filled, to maintain an appearance of balance it usually selects the already legitimized spokesperson for the downtrodden. Consistent with its focus on elites, *Nightline* seems to see Jackson as the "elite" of the alternative viewpoints.

The leading guests on programs covering social issues were Jerry Falwell (8), Cal Thomas (5) and Arthur Miller of Harvard Law School (5). Certainly, these numbers can partly be accounted for by the frequency of programs on TV evangelism in 1987. Still, the fact that Jerry Falwell and Cal Thomas, both closely associated with the right-wing Moral Majority, are two of *Nightline*'s three leading interpreters of social issues—speaking on such issues as crime and AIDS along with religion—is another indication of *Nightline*'s narrow range of guests.

ELITES

An examination of the occupations of the guests also yields interesting findings. As Figure 3.3 indicates, *Nightline*'s top-down approach results in disproportionate representation of elites.

In total, public interest, labor and racial/ethnic leaders comprised only 6.2 percent of the guests. When we look at U.S. guests only, 5.7 percent were labor, public interest and racial/ethnic leaders. In terms of certifying spokespersons, *Nightline* clearly does not cultivate the same types of relationships with these people as it does with people such as Kissinger, Haig and Falwell. No labor leader appeared more than twice. Of the public interest spokespersons, only Jesse Jackson and Richard Emery of the ACLU (5) appeared more than three times. Of the racial/ethnic leaders, 80 percent were foreign (mostly Black South Africans). Beyond Jesse Jackson, no U.S. racial/ethnic leader appeared more than three times.[9]

If we look at these data in more detail, we find interesting trends. On international issues, 54 percent of the guests were government officials and 6 percent were labor, public interest or racial/ethnic leaders. On the specific areas of the world that were central foreign policy issues—Central America, US-Soviet relations, the Persian Gulf—the percentage of government officials was in the 70 percent range. One could argue that the more important and controversial an issue is, the less diversity there is among *Nightline*'s guests.

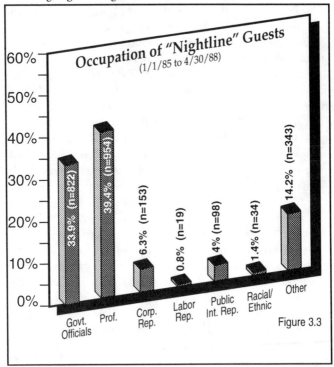

Occupation of "Nightline" Guests
(1/1/85 to 4/30/88)

- Govt. Officials: 33.6% (n=822)
- Prof.: 39.4% (n=954)
- Corp. Rep.: 6.3% (n=153)
- Labor Rep.: 0.8% (n=19)
- Public Int. Rep.: 4% (n=98)
- Racial/Ethnic: 1.4% (n=34)
- Other: 14.2% (n=343)

Figure 3.3

On shows about the economy, *Nightline* is heavily weighted towards private enterprise ideology: 37 percent of the guests were corporate representatives; 17 percent of the guests were government officials. Only 5 percent of the guests on shows about the economy were labor representatives. In general, cor-

about the economy were labor representatives. In general, corporate representatives comprised a large plurality, while public interest leaders were practically nonexistent. This is consistent with *Nightline*'s certification of elites as spokespeople.

On a more positive note, 26 percent of the guests on programs about South Africa were racial/ethnic leaders. This is, by far, the largest concentration of racial/ethnic leaders in our study. Given the subject matter it is not surprising. But government officials still made up a plurality (35 percent) of the guests.

Elites are not only featured on the program more often, they also speak more often than other guests. For example, the government officials averaged one fourth more lines spoken per guest (59), as measured in the transcripts, than public interest (48) and labor leaders (45). When labor and public interest spokespersons did manage to get on *Nightline*, they were likely to have less of an opportunity to speak than government officials.

In addition, elites were more likely to appear early in the program, the crucial time when they can help to frame the discussion that follows. Government officials, professionals and corporate representatives had an early appearance rate (.13) which was almost double that of public interest and labor leaders (.07).[10]

WHO APPEARS ALONE?

Seventy-four *Nightline* programs featured only one guest. Forty-nine of these (66 percent) were programs about international affairs, and 8 of these focused on U.S.-Soviet relations, the largest of any single topic. Not surprisingly, given *Nightline*'s reliance on elites, 90.5 percent of those solo guests were men; and 66 percent were current or former government or military officials. Other than Jesse Jackson, none of the guests who appeared alone were labor or public interest leaders.

Twelve individuals appeared on *Nightline* alone more than one time: Corazon Aquino (3), Jimmy Carter (3), Zbigniew Brzezinski (2), Gary Hart (2), Jesse Jackson (2), Henry Kissinger (2), Ferdinand Marcos (2), Robert McFarlane (2), Shimon Peres (2), Yitzhak Rabin (2), Richard Secord (2),

terns established by the larger figures: present and former U.S. government officials, high ranking foreign leaders, and Jesse Jackson. As an "elite" representative, Jesse Jackson is the only alternative U.S. voice among those repeat guests who appeared alone.

The entire list of solo guests includes such names as Alexander Haig, Caspar Weinberger, George Shultz, Jeane Kirkpatrick and William Westmoreland, and reads like a virtual who's who of the U.S. foreign policy establishment. On the other hand, the only outspoken progressive U.S. voice, other than Jesse Jackson, was author Studs Terkel.

Nightline had a broad range of foreign guests, including Daniel Ortega, Pik Botha, Robert Mugabe, and Rajiv Gandhi, who appeared alone. But guests from the U.S. who were afforded the opportunity to appear alone on *Nightline* represent a narrow spectrum of opinion. Articulate leaders of popular movements or the public interest community—such as Ralph Nader, Eleanor Smeal, Cesar Chavez, Randall Forsberg, Barry Commoner, Faye Wattleton, William Sloane Coffin, Michael Harrington, Randall Robinson, Frances Moore Lappe, to name only a few—were not deemed important enough to merit the undivided attention of *Nightline*'s viewers.

RACE AND GENDER

Nightline's propensity to draw heavily upon elite representatives of the status quo had negative consequences for race and gender representation on the show. As Figures 3.4 and 3.5 show, 90 percent of the guests were men and 83 percent for whom race was identifiable were white. Of U.S. guests, 89 percent were men and 92 percent were white.

On international issues, 94 percent of the guests were men. The only category which had a substantially better representation of women was social issues, and even here only 19 percent of the guests were women. Forty-one percent of the women who appeared on *Nightline* did so on programs about social issues, as compared to only 22 percent who appeared for discussions of international issues. By participating much more often on pro-

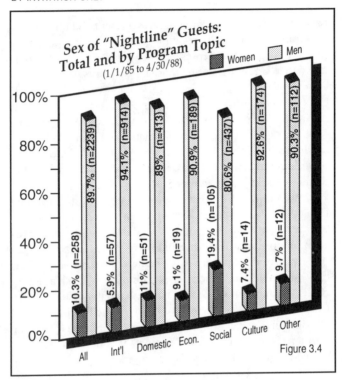

Sex of "Nightline" Guests:
Total and by Program Topic
(1/1/85 to 4/30/88)

■ Women □ Men

| | All | Int'l | Domestic | Econ. | Social | Culture | Other |

Women: 10.3% (n=258), 5.9% (n=57), 11% (n=51), 9.1% (n=19), 19.4% (n=105), 7.4% (n=14), 9.7% (n=12)

Men: 89.7% (n=2239), 94.1% (n=914), 89% (n=413), 90.9% (n=189), 80.6% (n=437), 92.6% (n=174), 90.3% (n=112)

Figure 3.4

grams about social issues than international or domestic political/economic issues, women who managed to get on *Nightline* were ghettoized into traditionally "female" areas.

The two leading women guests were Jeane Kirkpatrick (5) and Corazon Aquino (4), a right-wing former government official and a U.S.-allied foreign leader. Given *Nightline*'s primary interest in elite leaders, especially conservative ones, it is not surprising that none of the many women who have assumed leadership roles in public interest groups and peace organizations have appeared regularly on *Nightline*. For example, on shows about Central America, there was not one woman guest. This is largely a reflection of *Nightline*'s lack of attention to the U.S. movement against intervention in Central America which has many women in significant leadership roles.

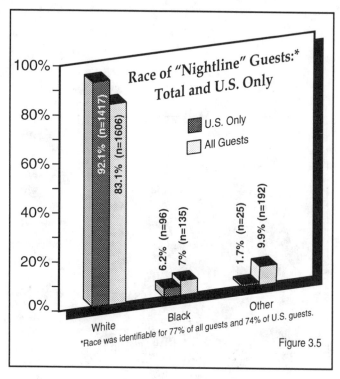

Race of "Nightline" Guests:*
Total and U.S. Only

White — 92.1% (n=1417) U.S. Only, 83.1% (n=1606) All Guests
Black — 6.2% (n=96) U.S. Only, 7% (n=135) All Guests
Other — 1.7% (n=25) U.S. Only, 9.9% (n=192) All Guests

*Race was identifiable for 77% of all guests and 74% of U.S. guests.

Figure 3.5

many women in significant leadership roles.

The fact that there are so few women on *Nightline* is clearly connected to the elite positions of most of the guests. Of the government officials, professionals and corporate representatives who appear, less than 10 percent were women. On the other hand, 16 percent of the labor leaders and 18 percent of the public interest representatives were women. Because there are so few public interest and labor representatives on *Nightline*, there are very few women as well. This suggests that *Nightline* does not systematically exclude women and minorities solely because of their race and gender, but also because women and minorities are disproportionately underrepresented in the class from which *Nightline* draws most of its guests.

Finally, an analysis of *Nightline* transcripts reveals that men

14 percent less, only 43 lines. Not only did men appear much more often, they also had more of an opportunity to speak.

On the whole, *Nightline* serves as an electronic soapbox from which white, male, elite representatives of the status quo can present their case. Minorities, women, and those with challenging views are generally excluded. The result is a portrait of remarkable domestic consensus versus seemingly endless foreign conflict. An examination of seven distinct issue areas will show in more detail how this portrait is developed.

Case Studies

A. The Soviet Union and US-Soviet Relations

Nightline's coverage of U.S. relations with the former Soviet Union provides a good example of the program's recurring tendency to limit the debate to "official" and "expert" spokespeople, while excluding viewpoints that dissent from those of government officials.

The Soviet Union was an important subject for *Nightline*. Nearly one in five (18.1 percent) guests on *Nightline*'s international programs were asked to discuss either the Soviet Union or US-Soviet relations. While the amount of coverage of US-Soviet relations varied in the 40 months studied, coverage of the Soviet Union steadily increased between 1985 and 1987.

It is revealing to look at the elite composition of the guest list for programs on either US-Soviet relations or the USSR. For programs on US-Soviet relations, nearly half of the guests (48.6 percent) were current or former U.S. officials, and 18.7 percent were foreign government officials. The most frequent U.S. guests, with three appearances each, were Henry Kissinger, Nixon's Secretary of State; Zbigniew Brzezinski, Carter's National Security Advisor and later of the Bush campaign; Robert McNamara, Defense Secretary under Kennedy and Johnson; Kenneth Adelman, Director of U.S. Arms Control and Disarmament Agency; and William Hyland, former NSC member and editor of the conservative journal *Foreign Affairs*. The U.S. perspective is represented by white, male, predominantly conservative elites. Top Soviet guests were Alexander Palladin

(Washington bureau chief of *Izvestia*), Gennadi Gerasimov (Soviet Foreign Ministry spokesperson), and Vitaly Churkin (Soviet Embassy First Secretary).

On programs dealing with the Soviet Union, rather than U.S.- Soviet relations, almost half of the guests (45.5 percent) were professionals (mostly academics, 27.3 percent, and journalists, 15.2 percent), one-fourth of the guests (24.2 percent) were U.S. government officials, and 9.1 percent of the guests were foreign government officials.

The most frequent guests were Harvard's Marshall Goldman (usually introduced as an "expert" on the Soviet Union), and Dimitri Simes (another "expert") from the Carnegie Endowment for International Peace, each with three appearances. (Simes' expertise is such that at a 1985 seminar soon after Gorbachev assumed power he predicted little would change in the USSR.) William Hyland (NSC, *Foreign Affairs*) and Gennadi Gerasimov each appeared twice.

The actions of each country's government and the sports-like rituals of the "superpower summits" dominate *Nightline*'s coverage of the Soviet Union and US-Soviet relations. The debate is framed primarily by representatives from two elite groups—the U.S. government and the Soviet government. Consequently, government officials dominate the guest list, while strong critics of government policy and representatives of the U.S. peace movement, as well as supporters of "unofficial" peace groups in Eastern Europe, are completely excluded. Instead, U.S.-Soviet relations are reported as an intricate game of diplomacy complete with a "Summit Scorecard," as an April 1985 program was titled.

The preoccupation with the "diplomatic game" results in *Nightline*'s devoting more than one-third of its shows on U.S.-Soviet relations to covering summits. Introducing a program on the 1985 Geneva summit news blackout, Koppel commented (11/20/85), "For the 3,500 reporters in Geneva it's still a game. Analyzing smiles, trying to read the tea leaves." *Nightline* was perhaps at the forefront of this elaborate game.

Consider this series of programs in 1985: "Kissinger: What

to Expect in Geneva" (1/4); "Geneva Talks: Why Did the Russians Come?" (1/7); "U.S. and Soviets: Let's Keep Talking" (1/8); "Kremlin Changeover: What Impact on Geneva?" (3/11); "Summit Scorecard" (4/10); "Geneva, Finally" (11/18); "Geneva: High Tech Desires" (11/19); "Geneva: The News Blackout" (11/20); "After the Summit" (11/21). *Nightline*, too, spends a great deal of time asking reporters, government officials, and "experts" to analyze smiles and read tea leaves.

The participants in these discussions reflect a narrow portion of the political spectrum. For example, on January 8, 1985, Koppel introduced his three guests this way: "Tonight, live from Geneva, the two Richards, Perle and Burt—Perle, the Pentagon hardliner, Burt, the State Department moderate. They will tell us how and why the U.S. and the Soviets have agreed to resume arms talks. And another view of the arms control talks and the latest White House staff realignment from a man who knows the ins and outs of both, former White House Chief of Staff and former Secretary of State Alexander Haig."

This is *Nightline*'s conception of a range of opinion: a Pentagon hardliner, a so-called State Department moderate, followed by Al Haig. This kind of "debate" leaves intact virtually every Reagan administration assumption about foreign policy. Any notion of a left or even liberal critique is missing. Inclusion of representatives from the U.S. or European peace movements would be so unusual for *Nightline* as to be startlingly radical. Richard Burt, a Cruise missile proponent, is a moderate for *Nightline*.

A problem with *Nightline*'s regular panels pitting U.S. administration officials against the Soviets is the implication that the United States speaks with a single voice—the administration's voice. As the massive nuclear freeze movement of the 1980's showed, this was not the case. Debates over U.S. policy between disarmament and Reagan administration spokespersons should have been common on TV forums. But they didn't happen on *Nightline*.

The limitation of discussion to the safe confines of those already in power was evident when the *Nightline* staff undertook a series of special programs that were broadcast simultaneously in the Soviet Union. The series was titled "Capital to Capital" and featured, exclusively, government officials speaking to each other. Alternative voices were not presented.

Even when examining ABC's controversial "Amerika" miniseries, Ted Koppel's "Viewpoint" panel (2/23/87) excluded the peace movement critics who had sparked the loudest reaction to a program in TV history. These voices were relegated to the tightly controlled environment of the taped introductory background story.

A similar process of confinement and exclusion is evident in *Nightline*'s coverage of the Soviet Union, as opposed to U.S.-Soviet relations. It should be noted that *Nightline* often features programs on the Soviet government's use of media to communicate (read: propagandize) its views. Shows such as "Mikhail Gorbachev's PR" (10/1/85), "Gorbachev and the Media" (10/3/85), "Chernobyl: Openness or Propaganda?" (5/14/86), "The New Soviet Media Campaign" (8/27/86), and "Soviet Spokesmen" (3/5/87) call into question Soviet government officials' attempts to influence media coverage. Yet similar PR campaigns waged by U.S. government officials are rarely if ever scrutinized on *Nightline*. In *Nightline*'s view, the Soviet Foreign Ministry provides "propagandists," while the U.S. State Department serves up foreign policy "experts" like Elliott Abrams and Otto Reich.

B. Terrorism

The problem of terrorism has been a frequent focus of *Nightline*'s coverage since the program began as "The Iran Crisis: America Held Hostage." Its continued focus on the terrorist threat and the tone of its coverage often gives the impression that the United States is under siege.

Nightline's coverage of terrorism starts with the premise that acts of terrorism are committed against "us"—the "us" usually meaning the United States, but it can be expanded to include our allies or the "Western world." The kind of terrorism that *Nightline* pays attention to are acts of terror committed by small groups on planes, ships, at airports—what Edward Herman has described as "retail terror."[11] Yet, *Nightline* never focused on regular and routine state terror—or "wholesale terror" as Herman calls it—which occurred daily during the period of this study with the assistance of U.S. dollars, weapons, and sometimes training in countries like El Salvador and Guatemala. This kind of terrorism, which takes many times more lives each year, does not exist in *Nightline*'s worldview.

Nightline avoids coverage of U.S.-backed state terror by excluding guests who might attempt to reframe the discussion in a way that addresses all forms of terrorism, including death squad activity in El Salvador and disappearances in Guatemala and Honduras. By ignoring U.S.-backed state terror, *Nightline* turns terrorism into an "us" versus "them" scenario. *Nightline*'s view seems to be: They are terrorists; we are the targets.

The geographic focus of *Nightline*'s terrorism coverage is worth exploring. Forty-eight percent of the 52 *Nightline* programs on terrorism were related to the Middle East. The implication of such selective coverage is that Arabs are far and away the primary cause of terrorism in the world. The fact that *Nightline* is really only interested in terrorism when it happens in the context of the Middle East—and not when it happens elsewhere in the world—is significant.

When we examine the types of guests who appear on *Nightline* shows about terrorism, the limited picture becomes even more evident. Even more than other topics, *Nightline* programs about terrorism were male dominated: 95 percent of the guests were men. The programs were also dominated by official sources and experts. Forty-five percent of the guests were government officials and 46 percent were professionals. A total of 91 percent of the guests represent elite opinion. Jesse Jackson was the only public interest spokesperson; only one percent of the guests were labor representatives (e.g., airline pilots discussing security); and three percent were racial/ethnic leaders.

In short, *Nightline* maintains a top-down approach when it comes to dealing with its number one threat: terrorism. Excluded are victims of wholesale state terror and those who are actively resisting state terror in the Third World, as well as analysts who might articulate the frustration and anger that fosters terrorism. Also excluded are domestic critics of the U.S. government's (and *Nightline*'s) conceptualization of terrorism. A more inclusive approach would find these voices as significant as those of the U.S. power elite.

An examination of the individual guests who appeared on the programs about terrorism also paints an interesting picture. Benjamin Netanyahu, Israel's' Ambassador to the U.N. and author of the book, *Terrorism: How the West Can Win*, was the most frequent commentator, appearing five times. Perhaps this is because Israel has been the direct or indirect target of much of the terrorism which *Nightline* chooses to cover. Another explanation is that the Israeli government in general, and Netanyahu in particular, calls for a tough response to terrorism, in keeping with the kind of terrorist crisis which *Nightline* depicts.

Following Netanyahu in frequency of appearance, at four times each, were Henry Kissinger, whose views are similar to those of Netanyahu, and Said Rajaie-Khorassani, the Iranian Ambassador to the U.N. The fact that Kissinger is a regular guest is no surprise, given that *Nightline* promotes him as the leading expert on many, if not most, international issues.

Ambassador Rajaie's appearances are noteworthy, for here *Nightline* gives voice to a different, non-western perspective. Yet, regardless of whether the attempts are sincere (one might suggest that this is *Nightline*'s attempt to present someone considered to be a supporter of terrorism), the results hardly detract from the Kissinger-Netanyahu worldview. In fact, selecting Rajaie as the main "alternative" spokesperson on terrorism helps to strengthen this worldview, while reinforcing the notion that alternative views on terrorism are literally foreign.

Other guests who appeared three or more times on shows about terrorism were Abdallah Bouhabib, Lebanese Ambassador to the U.S.; Alexander Haig; Brian Jenkins of the RAND corporation; Ambassador Clovis Maksoud from the Arab League; State Department consultant Michael Ledeen who was involved in the Reagan administration's secret arms shipments to Iran; Noel Koch, former assistant secretary of defense in charge of counter-terrorism; and Robert Kupperman of the Georgetown Center for Strategic and International Studies.

These guests, including three men who were at one time or another involved in the Reagan-Bush administration's foreign policy making, are part of a familiar pattern. Ambassadors Bouhabib and Maksoud appeared on *Nightline* to discuss specific acts of terrorism (i.e., a hijacking) occurring in the Middle East; they were not chosen to explore the roots or potential solutions to the broader problem of terrorism. Again the only views which hint at an alternative understanding are those of foreigners.

Nightline's six most frequent U.S. commentators on terrorism were Kissinger, Haig and four "terrorism experts." All are hard-nosed cold warriors who emphasize "counter-terrorism." Their views are essentially the same—whether it be about how to respond to terrorism, or how to define the key issues when discussing terrorism.

When the discussion focuses on how the U.S. should deal with the terrorist threat, the regulars are there to tell us. For example, after the hijackers of the Achille Lauro were captured, Henry Kissinger and Israeli Defense Minister Yitzhak Rabin appeared on *Nightline* to tell us what measures we should take in response to terrorism. During the April 1988 hijacking of a Kuwaiti airplane, Noel Koch and Brian Jenkins provided analysis of how to deal with the situation. In both cases, the spectrum of opinion was so narrow it may be misleading to call it a spectrum.

Terrorism is a topic which provokes some of the more extremist (and, in light of Iran/contra revelations, some of the more hypocritical) foreign policy rhetoric, often at the expense of an examination of the complexities of the issue. As far as *Nightline* is concerned, the United States speaks with only one voice when it comes to terrorism. There is no serious disagreement (except for the couple of times that Jesse Jackson appeared) when it comes to terrorism. There is also little discussion of the definition of terrorism, the conditions that foster it, or of the countries arguably responsible for most of the world's terrorism. In short, *Nightline*'s discussion of the issue reflects and reinforces a worldview that is strikingly similar to the policies of the Reagan-Bush administration.

C. Southern Africa

Southern Africa is another area to which *Nightline* pays a good deal of attention. In fact, it is essentially the only part of Africa that *Nightline* keeps abreast of regularly. A major shortcoming of *Nightline*'s Southern Africa coverage was its isolated nature. The coverage was almost exclusively focused on South Africa; there was little or no discussion of other countries in the region, including Namibia, Angola, Mozambique, or Zimbabwe. *Nightline* approaches South Africa as if it can be understood outside of a regional context.

Despite its tendency toward fragmentation, *Nightline*'s coverage of South Africa is perhaps its strongest suit. In contrast to programs on other foreign policy issues, 45 percent of the guests were black—by far the largest representation of people of color on any issue. On the 35 shows, with 88 guests during the time of this study, over one-fourth of the guests (26 percent) were racial/ethnic leaders. Again, this was the largest representation of racial/ethnic leaders on any issue, as *Nightline* generally did a relatively good job of including the views of black South Africans. Still, less than 7 percent of the guests on these programs were women.

The most frequent guest on shows about South Africa was Bishop Desmond Tutu, with five appearances. Given the fact that Tutu was awarded the Nobel Peace Prize in 1984, and Ted Koppel once proclaimed Tutu as "perhaps the best known spokesman" for black South Africans, his regular appearances are not surprising. It is consistent with *Nightline*'s tendency to rely on well known personalities to provide analysis.

Right behind Tutu in frequency of appearance, with four each, were Pik Botha, Louis Nel, Herbert Beukes and Nthato Motlana. The first three were high ranking members of the

South African government and Motlana was a prominent black civic leader in Soweto. While it is impressive that *Nightline* had regular appearances from a second black South African, it's worth noting that 3 of the 5 most frequent guests were representatives of the South African government. Indeed, the appearances of the upholders of apartheid in combination with that of Tutu or Motlana made for some of the most informative and provocative programming. Were this type of balance applied to all issues, *Nightline* would be presenting a substantially broader picture of the world.

Nightline's coverage primarily featured the voices of South Africans, both black and white. Only 24 percent of the guests on *Nightline* programs about South Africa were from the United States. What is disconcerting is that the list of U.S. guests generally did not include representatives of the movement of Americans critical of apartheid and of U.S. government and corporate policy toward South Africa. While *Nightline* did a fairly good job of presenting debate among South Africans, the presentation of the debate in the U.S. left much to be desired. This is significant because *Nightline* is an important part of the political debate in the United States. While programs about South Africa and the continuing struggle there are important, the role of the United States and U.S. policy merits more attention on U.S. television than it receives.

Approximately one third, or 12 of the 35 programs on South Africa, dealt in some substantive way with U.S. policy. Only four guests appeared more than once on these programs: Chester Crocker (3), Pik Botha (2), Nthato Motlana (2) and Frank Wisner (2). Crocker was Assistant Secretary of State for African Affairs, and the chief architect of the Reagan Administration's policy of "constructive engagement." Frank Wisner was the Deputy Assistant Secretary of State for African Affairs, a top aide of Crocker's. Of the four remaining guests on programs which include a discussion of U.S. policy, two were from the Reagan administration, one from the South African government and one was a black South African. The list does not include any spokespersons for the anti-apartheid movement in this country, nor any opposition figures from the Democratic Party. Essentially, the analysts of U.S. policy were Crocker and Wisner, the ones making U.S. policy. While anti-apartheid voices from within the U.S. were occasionally aired on *Nightline*, they did not become a regular part of the debate the way apologists for apartheid did.

While aspects of *Nightline*'s South African coverage warrant praise, its limited perspective must also be questioned. Why does *Nightline* persist in portraying South Africa outside the context of the region, especially when it sponsored wars against neighboring countries for years? Why were representatives of the U.S. anti-apartheid movement, one of the largest social movements of the 1980's, not regular participants in the political debate over apartheid and U.S. policy toward South Africa? The fact that the Reagan administration, whose representatives figured prominently on *Nightline*, promoted an understanding of South Africa that ignored both the regional context and the anti-apartheid movement in the U.S. may provide a clue to answering these questions.

D. Central America

In our study period, *Nightline* presented 27 shows (68 guests) focusing on Central America. Of these programs, almost all dealt exclusively with Nicaragua. In a manner similar to the way South Africa was discussed in isolation, Nicaragua was typically covered as if the rest of Central America did not exist. The focus was on the government the U.S. opposes, its human rights record and alleged abuses of democracy. The same criteria of newsworthiness were not applied to the governments of Honduras, El Salvador and Guatemala, all of whom are closely allied with the U.S. and receive large sums of money from the U.S. government. These three governments had been condemned by independent human rights organizations for committing far worse abuses than Nicaragua, yet *Nightline* largely ignored Nicaragua's neighbors.

The fact that the Reagan administration had little interest in publicizing violations in El Salvador, Honduras and Guatemala, while at the same time running a propaganda war against the Nicaraguan government, may help to explain *Nightline*'s fixation on Nicaragua. In selecting which Central America stories to cover, *Nightline* seemed to follow the agenda set by the Reagan administration.

No one would deny that the Nicaraguan government committed abuses; certainly it did. But Nicaragua's abuses paled in comparison to El Salvador, Honduras, and Guatemala, the so-called "fledgling democracies" of Central America. This fundamental point was obscured by *Nightline*'s isolated and fragmented picture of the region. While 22 *Nightline* programs dealt principally with Nicaragua, not one focused principally on El Salvador, Honduras or Guatemala.

Debate about Nicaragua was almost always framed in terms of how the U.S. should deal with the Sandinistas. Should it try to overthrow the government overtly or covertly? Should it put pressure on them militarily, politically, or economically? *Nightline*'s coverage of the late-1980's peace process assumed that Nicaragua was the primary obstacle to peace in the region and that it did not plan to abide by any agreement and therefore needed to be pressured. These assumptions greatly limit the terms of the discussion. The fact that Nicaragua is an impoverished country of three million people defending itself against military intervention by the most powerful country in the world was seemingly irrelevant. Condemnation of U.S. policy by the World Court and by most of the countries of Latin America also seemed to be irrelevant.

When we look at the most frequent guests we find Alejandro Bendana (11) from the Nicaraguan foreign ministry; Elliott Abrams (7) of the State Department; and Senator Christopher Dodd (6). At first glance this might indicate a good balance. After all, Bendana articulately put forth the Nicaraguan position, Abrams defended U.S. policy and Dodd was critical of U.S. policy. Yet, this is only a good balance if we accept the assumptions which *Nightline* begins with; once we broaden the picture to include more than just a discussion of how to overthrow or pressure Nicaragua, the semblance of balance vanishes.

More specifically, U.S. opponents of intervention in Central America were given virtually no voice. In forty months, only two guests (out of 68) were anti-intervention spokespersons (less than 3 percent). Given that the anti-intervention movement was one of the most prominent opposition movements of the 1980's, the fact that movement leaders were not represented is significant. Instead, 78 percent of the guests on *Nightline*'s programs about Central America were government officials (55 percent U.S. officials).

All the guests on *Nightline*'s Central America programs were men, and 69 percent of the guests were from the U.S. Whereas the lack of representation of the domestic anti-apartheid movement is partially explained by the program's focus on foreign guests as opposed to U.S. guests, no such explanation can be found with respect to Central America. The great majority of guests were from the U.S., but still the vast numbers of U.S. citizens opposing U.S. policy were virtually unrepresented.

What we see instead is a procession of conservative ideologues, whether they be congressmen like Gordon Humphreys, Henry Hyde, and Richard Cheney; or members of the Administration like Elliott Abrams and Otto Reich; or activists like John Silber, John Singlaub or Richard Secord. Nicaragua was one of the pet issues of the American Right; *Nightline*'s Central America coverage provided a regular platform for cold war ideologues to fulminate about "the communist threat on our continent."

An analysis of the thirteen *Nightline* programs which substantively discuss U.S. policy in the region discloses that the most frequent guests are Elliott Abrams (4), John Singlaub (3), Christopher Dodd (3) and Alejandro Bendana (3). Again, Abrams and Singlaub put forward the usual anti-communist rhetoric; Dodd accepted much of the rhetoric and played the role of insider opponent, disagreeing on specific administration tactics without challenging the underlying assumptions of the policy (i.e., that the U.S. seeks to bring "democracy" to Nicaragua); and Bendana represented the "enemy" we were waging war against.

The participation of Bendana, a forthright critic of U.S. policy, is in line with *Nightline*'s practice of presenting the views of controversial foreign leaders. But prominent U.S. citizens who sought a fundamental change in U.S. policy were not on *Nightline*'s guest list. U.S. policy, after all, should be subjected to a U.S. debate; a robust, full-spectrum debate did not occur on *Nightline*.

Several examples illustrate how *Nightline* tilted the discussion rightward. On three programs about contra aid (one each from 1986, '87 and '88), *Nightline* had the following set of guests: Patrick Buchanan and Tom Wicker; General John Singlaub and Senator David Boren; and Alfredo Cesar, Robert Owen, John Singlaub and Rep. David Bonior. In the first case, Buchanan, a committed right-wing ideologue who helped promote the contra movement, debated Wicker, a liberal journalist who is in no way connected to the movement opposing U.S. policy in Central America. In the second case, John Singlaub, another right-wing ideologue who was affiliated with the World Anti-Communist League and the contra cause, debated Senator David Boren, a Democrat who had voted in favor of military aid to the contras. In the final case, contra leader Alfredo Cesar and contra arms suppliers Robert Owen and John Singlaub appeared with Rep. David Bonior, a Democrat who opposed military aid to the contras. (On this program, Koppel failed to ask Owen about his memos to Oliver North describing contra leaders as corrupt drug runners and U.S. pawns.) In each of the aforementioned cases, only part of the national debate was presented. Forthright opponents of U.S. policy in Central America were excluded.

Nightline's coverage of Central America was also decidedly ahistorical. Koppel and his guests paid little attention to the historic role the U.S. government has played in the region, except for obligatory comments about "our commitment to democracy." Nor was the war against Nicaragua discussed in the context of either Nicaragua's history or prior destabilization campaigns run by the U.S. against governments in such countries as Guatemala, Chile and Cuba.

In sum, *Nightline*'s coverage on Central America scrutinized Nicaragua in isolation from the region, offered little or no historical context, and provided right-wing ideologues with a regular soapbox, while excluding spokespeople for the U.S. anti-intervention movement. This was exactly the kind of picture that the U.S. government tried to paint: one that has no comparative or historical context, but is overflowing with anti-communist rhetoric. The result is a vision of Central America that confuses and obfuscates, which was one of the central goals of the Reagan administration's propaganda campaign.

E. Media and Politics

Between January 1985 and April 1988, 3.2 percent of *Nightline* guests appeared on programs that examined the media's role in society. These programs were of two types. The majority of them were programs in the traditional *Nightline* format dealing with journalism and current trends in media coverage. Revelations about Gary Hart's personal conduct that ended his presidential candidacy resulted in five separate *Nightline* programs on either the press' role in the Hart incident or, more generally, on the problems involved in covering the private lives of public figures. After Ariel Sharon and William Westmoreland each sued major media for libel, *Nightline* devoted three shows to their cases and, more generally, to the issue of libel suits. Other programs of this type covered traditional topics such as the protection of journalists' sources.

The *Nightline* staff produced a second type of media program purporting to offer self-critical examinations of the kind of job the media are doing. These special expanded "Viewpoint" programs were hosted by Ted Koppel in front of live audiences.

In both types of programs, journalists dominate the guest list (55.7 percent). Current and former government and military officials make up nearly another fifth (19 percent) of the guests, while corporate representatives have the third highest representation (6.3 percent). Academics (1.3 percent) and public interest representatives (2.6 percent) make up only a tiny fraction of the guests. Hence what we usually see is journalists

evaluating journalists. A better way of assessing media performance might be to feature critical perspectives from the public
interest and academic communities.

As in other cases we examined, a vast majority of guests on
programs dealing with media and politics were white (95.5 percent) American (97.5 percent) males (90 percent). Comments
from women, minorities, public interest representatives or foreign observers were grossly neglected and often completely
absent.

In this study, which criticizes *Nightline*'s programming, it is
germane to look at how the show deals with criticism. Which
criticism does *Nightline* (and ABC News) recognize and which
criticism does it ignore? These questions require a closer look,
in particular, at the "Viewpoint" programs.[12]

On April 17, 1985 Ted Koppel introduced a "Viewpoint"
program on patriotism and the media by saying that
"'Viewpoint' is our periodic examination of the media and how
we are perceived by you, our audience, our critics." But to which
critics does Koppel pay attention? Our analysis of "Viewpoint"
transcripts suggests that they are overwhelmingly conservative.
For example, the only advocates on the media and patriotism
panel were conservative ones: James Watt, former Secretary of
the Interior; William Rusher, publisher of the conservative
National Review; and the Republican representative Philip
Crane.

Jeff Greenfield's introductory piece for this program featured a notable quote from Ted Turner, who at the time was
apparently allied with a right-wing bid to take over CBS. "In my
opinion," said Turner, "the greatest enemies that America has
ever had, posing a greater threat to our way of life than Nazi
Germany or Tojo's Japan, are the three television networks and
the people that run them who are living amongst us and con-
stantly tearing down everything that has made this country
great." Other quotes from the piece came from Arnaud de
Borchgrave, right-wing editor of the *Washington Times*; Defense
Secretary Caspar Weinberger; and ultra-conservative Reed
Irvine of Accuracy in Media. The only critic quoted who was not

a strong conservative was Michael Massing of the *Columbia Journalism Review*.

The ideology of this particular program was especially blatant. Other less blatant programs also presented "debates" between conservative critics and journalists, leaving out the progressive segment of the political spectrum. Questions from "Viewpoint"'s invited audiences which, Koppel once claimed, "represent a wide spectrum of political opinion," also were usually from a conservative standpoint.

Only occasionally was a progressive critic invited. Alexander Cockburn of *The Nation* appeared twice on these programs. In a show asking "Is the Media Too One-Sided?" Cockburn was paired off against right-winger Arnaud de Borchgrave of the *Washington Times*. Unlike conservatives, progressive critics never dominated a panel; instead they were scrupulously matched against right-wing ideologues. This gives the media an out: "If both the left and the right are criticizing us," some journalists will rationalize, "we must be doing a great job."

In the end, *Nightline*'s supposed self-examination may merely reinforce the show's longstanding self-perception. As Koppel argued on one "Viewpoint" (7/30/85), ABC News is "acknowledging not necessarily that we have done wrong but that many of you in our audience are firmly convinced that we have done wrong." By responding primarily to the much ballyhooed, but undocumented "leftwing bias" critique lodged by conservatives while avoiding progressive critics (such as Ben Bagdikian, Noam Chomsky, Pat Aufderheide, or Michael Parenti), "Viewpoint" programs have become part of a self-affirming ritual that allows journalists to ignore criticisms, unless they come from those in power.

Indeed, criticisms from those not wielding power—the left, women, labor, minorities, public interest groups, etc.— were hardly given an opportunity to be heard. In the *Nightline* tradition of top- down journalism, the media critique which is heard comes from the segment of society that wields power and, at best, aims to maintain the status quo under a conservative administration. Ignored is the critique voiced by those outside the corridors of power who call for change in American society.

F. Economy

Nightline's economic coverage followed the pattern of elites discussing an issue—on which there is apparent domestic consensus—from a perspective closely aligned with that of the U.S. government. The elites in *Nightline*'s economic coverage were members of the business community. As it turns out, much of *Nightline*'s economic coverage is essentially coverage of U.S. business. While the show's economic coverage spanned a range of topics, nearly one-fifth (19.7 percent) of economic programs focused on the stock market. Labor received the attention of only 7.2 percent of the programs.

Labor was grossly underrepresented in *Nightline*'s economic coverage even though labor, not the business community, represents the bulk of active participants in our economy. More than one out of three (37 percent) guests on economic programs represented the business community, but only one in twenty (5.3 percent) represented labor. Other guests included government officials (15.4 percent) academics (13.9 percent) and journalists (12 percent). Labor was outnumbered by both journalists and academics by more than two to one; by government officials, three to one; and by corporate representatives, seven to one.[13]

The generally conservative business voice overpowered labor and public interest concerns in more ways than just sheer numbers. Corporate representatives were nearly three times as likely as labor leaders to appear before the first commercial break, thus enabling corporate spokespersons to set the agenda for the program's discussion.

While the guest list for business and economic programs was not dominated by key individuals to the extent that we found in other categories, there are some repeat appearances worth noting. Irwin Jacobs, corporate raider and chairperson of MINSTAR, and then-professor Robert Reich of Harvard each appeared four times during the period studied. Monte Gordon, vice president and director of research for the Dreyfus Corporation and Arthur Laffer, supply-side economics guru of the Reagan administration, each appeared three times. Except for Reich, the most frequent guests on programs about the economy were of a conservative bent.

Nightline's economic coverage, like much of its international coverage, is focused on the elites. In international coverage *Nightline* tends to have government officials talking to government officials about government policies. On economics, business executives and analysts talk to other business executives and analysts about the latest business trends. Absent is any continuing discussion of the effect of corporate action on communities and constituencies other than the business community. Programs on workers, instead of flashy merger moguls, were rarely seen on *Nightline.*

Given the dominance of corporate representatives and the gross underrepresentation of labor, it is not surprising to discover that the range of debate on economic issues on *Nightline* is rather narrow. Legitimate positions recognized by *Nightline* fall squarely within the dominant U.S. capitalist frame. Challengers, even those suggesting only moderate reform of the current economic order, were virtually nonexistent on *Nightline*'s guest list.

Also absent was any analysis of corporate America as a political force in the world. For a program which prides itself on international coverage, *Nightline*'s economic reporting was grossly U.S.-centered and out of touch with the realities of our international economy. A full 89.4 percent of programs on the economy focused on the United States, and 94.2 percent of the guests were from the U.S.

It is impossible to understand international relations without examining U.S. corporate actions and economic interests abroad. Yet *Nightline*'s business and economic coverage does not inform its international coverage. *Nightline*, as we have seen, provided virtually no analysis of U.S. corporate influence and control abroad—influence which is often a catalyst for political events (revolutions, military coups, etc.). This is yet another example of how *Nightline*'s coverage coincides with the interests of the U.S. government. Just as U.S. officials discuss politics as if it were divorced from economics, so too does *Nightline*'s coverage convey this impression.

G. Religion

Nightline's vision of religion was completely dominated by a particular phenomenon: televangelism. *Nightline* was a program which essentially ignored religion in 1985 and 1986. In 1985, it produced only four programs with religious topics; two of these were about the troubles of the Bhagwan Shree Rajneesh. In 1986, *Nightline* broadcast a single program on religion which featured no guests, entitled "Politics and Religion: Christian Fundamentalism."

In 1987, however, religion coverage increased dramatically as the PTL scandal broke. Suddenly, *Nightline* became interested in religion, broadcasting ten programs on the PTL and televangelism in just over two months. In all, 16 religion programs were broadcast in 1987 with 11 devoted to PTL/televangelism. In the first four months of 1988, another four programs were devoted to religious topics, and all of these dealt with televangelism.

With 64 percent of *Nightline*'s religious shows devoted to televangelists, more established forms of religion received comparatively little coverage. Catholics were featured in four programs, two of which covered the Pope's 1987 visit to the United States. As mentioned, Rajneesh had two shows, while Jews, Baptists and Fundamentalists were each the focus of one show.

The most frequent guests on religion programs were rightwing political activist and Moral Majority founder Jerry Falwell (seven appearances) and former Moral Majority vice president turned syndicated columnist Cal Thomas (four appearances). In addition to Rajneesh and *Newsweek*'s Kenneth Woodward, six other guests appeared twice on *Nightline*'s religion programs: Jim Bakker (PTL president), Rev. Everett Stenhouse (Assemblies of God, of which PTL is a part), Roy Grutman (PTL attorney), Mike Evans (Assemblies of God), Frances Kissling (Catholics for Free Choice), and Catholic Archbishop John Forbes.

Most of *Nightline*'s coverage had little to do with the impact of religion on our society, or the role of religion abroad. Instead it dwelt on flashy personalities and their "sexy" scandals. Jim and Tammy Bakker, Jerry Falwell and Jimmy Swaggart became the focal "personalities" of religion for supermarket tabloids and *Nightline* alike. The sensational PTL scandal was virtually the only time on *Nightline* that religion was deemed worthy of in-depth coverage.

In many ways, religion is a unique case in our analysis. Unlike the other case studies, it doesn't fit neatly in our analysis of elites, domestic consensus, and parallel agendas. What is most notable about *Nightline*'s coverage of religion is what it didn't cover.

It didn't cover in any detail the serious debates within religious denominations that are having a profound effect on many Americans. For example, the Catholic Church in the U.S. was publicly confronting a number of major issues including economic justice, the nuclear arms race, hunger in America, sanctuary for Central American refugees, and so on. Meanwhile, the Church itself was involved in vigorous internal debate over issues such as liberation theology, the role of women, abortion, homosexuality, divorce, birth control, and more. But *Nightline* did not see fit to focus on these issues during the period of our study. Protestants, Jews, Moslems and other religious observers grapple with similar issues, but *Nightline* ignored the concerns of millions of believers in this country.

The gossip-sheet type of coverage of the PTL scandal may have garnered high ratings, but it failed to probe the complex influence of religion on social and political life in America.

Putting the Pieces Together

As the ratings indicate, *Nightline* is a program that reaches and influences millions of Americans. The show has won two dozen Emmys for television news coverage, indicating that *Nightline* is influential within the industry. It is able to attract high ranking U.S. government officials as well as prestigious foreign leaders as guests, an indication that political leaders recognize the program's influence. Moreover, *Nightline* has managed to achieve its influential status in part through a process of self-certification.

It is clear not only from the general tone of the program, but also from its advertisements and introductory segments, that *Nightline* takes itself very seriously. It is not just entertainment, nor does it consider itself simply another news program. It presents itself as *the* television news program capable of dealing with serious issues and willing to feature controversial guests.

A 1988 commercial for the program highlighted a reviewer's rave that *Nightline* "may be simply the best program in the history of broadcast journalism." By touting its own qualifications, *Nightline* in essence certifies itself as an important player in domestic and world events.

More specifically, *Nightline* is organized in a way that sets Ted Koppel up as a "diplomat" to moderate discussions between two or more apparently antagonistic viewpoints. This is where *Nightline* presents itself as more than just TV news. The implication is that conflicts can be resolved just by having antagonists talk to each other on *Nightline*, via satellite, with Ted Koppel as the intermediary.

While *Nightline* often is successful at bringing together political opponents on the same program, its attempt to find a "solution" unmasks *Nightline*'s political perspective. If, indeed, there are solutions to be found, on what basis will they rest? With respect to foreign policy, the "solutions" Koppel seeks are essentially outcomes that the U.S. government finds desirable. When Koppel puts on the hat of diplomat and assumes the role more of statesperson than a journalist, it becomes evident that the worldview informing *Nightline*'s international coverage is little different from that of the U.S. government.[14]

Like most television news programs, *Nightline* holds itself out as providing as complete a picture of the world as possible, undistorted by subjective self-selection. Yet, when virtually all of *Nightline*'s Central America programs focused on the perceived shortcomings of Nicaragua—and not one focused on problems in El Salvador, Guatemala or Honduras—the selection process is unmistakable. And it seems more than coincidence that Nicaragua's misdeeds were high on the Reagan administration's agenda while those of its neighbors were not. The amount of overlap between *Nightline*'s worldview and the agenda of the U.S. government is one of the most disturbing findings of our study.

The Illusion of Balance

Nightline has a very good reputation within broadcast journalism. One of *Nightline*'s trademarks has been the controversial guests and lively discussions that are often part of the program. But despite the sometimes cantankerous debates between *Nightline*'s guests and its host, we conclude that the appearance of a "balance" among guests representing diverse perspectives is often more illusory than real.

As Gaye Tuchman has pointed out, TV news programs try to observe a balance norm, but this does not necessarily result in a real balance.[15] Usually, the official viewpoint is presented along with one "critical" view. Whether this is only one of many critical views, or even the most significant of the several critical perspectives does not matter. More often than not, the "critical" views are those of establishment insiders.

Nightline follows this norm, as well. Usually, though not always, it presents two sides of an issue. However, most stories have more than two sides. Certain perspectives, including those of U.S. progressives, are systematically excluded from *Nightline*.

If balance is having two people, usually elites or experts, disagreeing over fine points rather than a range of guests arguing fundamental questions, then *Nightline* presents a balanced guest list. In reality, *Nightline*'s observance of the balance norm obscures the fact that there are stark imbalances.

As we have noted earlier, the exclusion of progressive viewpoints occurs through the processes of legitimation, limitation, and certification. By legitimizing differing views within a narrow political spectrum, the appearance of balance is maintained while a process of limitation is obscured. Similarly, the range of spokespeople who are certified by *Nightline* is wide enough to enable "debates" to occur, yet limited enough to exclude those who might question the fundamental tenets of the status quo.

Noted journalist Bill Moyers,[16] quoting *Newsday*'s Tom Collins, has commented on this process: "'It's usually two experts out of the establishment who are called on this talk show or that talk show. It's usually a politician, a pollster, a pundit, or a quote, expert.' It's a very tiny sample of thought, of ideas, of language that gets on television.... There's another kingdom of thought out there that never gets tapped, that throws light, backlight, on the stage of politics.'"[17] This description is an apt one for *Nightline*.

Some of the "framing" processes which occur on *Nightline* are more subtle than the outright exclusion of alternative views. Instead, *Nightline* compartmentalizes alternative views. For the most part, truly critical views come from foreigners (read: un-American). This helps to reinforce the appearance of balance. We see foreign guests who are at times severely critical of the United States, and we see journalists and occasionally academics who provide us with a view that may differ from those in power. But the people who go beyond the bounds of establishment dissent and actively oppose the status quo are locked out of *Nightline*. The progressive public interest community is almost entirely invisible.[18] Certainly some representatives will appear on *Nightline* once in a great while, but on the issues that *Nightline* defines as important—international politics, for example—such views are difficult or impossible to find.

What we have then, is a program that both reflects and helps to define the limits of "reasonable" debate. When *Nightline* acts in this capacity as a gatekeeper, whether consciously or otherwise, it defines the world in a manner that coincides with the assumptions and premises of those who pull the levers of government and corporate power.

Fulfilling *Nightline's* Potential

After all is said, *Nightline* remains a program with great potential. The combination of its prestige, popularity, and ability to attract provocative guests means that it could become a truly informative and educational program.

In thinking of ways to improve *Nightline*, we echo some of Herbert Gans' suggestions for news media. First, *Nightline* would need to greatly diversify its guest list and move beyond the restrictive formula that equates national interest with the interest of the U.S. government. The program should regularly and systematically include representatives of citizen organizations, especially organizations which represent groups beyond the boundaries of the white, male, power establishment. Peace and public interest groups, unions, women's groups, church-based organizations, minority and civil rights groups, and other social movement organizations, to name a few, should be granted regular access to the arena of debate now so closely guarded by *Nightline*.

Second, this democratic broadening of the guest list should be accompanied by a similar broadening of the range of topics covered by *Nightline*. Programs should not only focus on the issues and countries which currently interest the U.S. government. Instead, deeper, more profound issues and changes in society should be examined, even if this means the loss of flashy or well-known personalities as guests. (It may well be that passionate advocates from the public interest community, even by ratings-oriented criteria, will prove more provocative and telegenic than the predictable players like Kissinger and Brzezinski.)

Third, international news should be set in both a regional and historical context, rather than the geographical and historical isolation which has usually been the case.

Above all, the program should focus less on the "selling" of U.S. foreign policy and more on providing various interpretations of, and a context for, important events and trends in everyday life. The fact that Koppel can make a statement about having the qualifications to "sell American foreign policy...to Congress [and] the American public" and not see a fundamental conflict of interest with his role as a journalist says more about the U.S. media than all the "Viewpoint" shows he has hosted.

What we suggest in this study is that certain views—particularly those of white, male "establishment" representatives—are more acceptable than others to *Nightline* and most media. Our analysis of 40 months of *Nightline* programming suggests that the media play a key role in maintaining the Washington-Wall Street structures of power. They serve this function by legitimizing a narrow range of political positions, limiting the "acceptable" scope of debate, and by certifying a small band of "experts."

The answer one gets to a question often depends on who one is asking. *Nightline* asks its questions primarily of Washington-Wall Street elites. It is not surprising, then, that the answers it broadcasts to the American public promote the interests of those elites.

4
All The Usual Suspects: *MacNeil/Lehrer* And *Nightline*

In February 1989 FAIR published our study, "Are You on the *Nightline* Guest List?" The study generated much discussion in the media and elsewhere. We chose *Nightline* for the first study because it is widely perceived to be the best that television journalism has to offer. However, our data showed that a narrow range of panelists dominated *Nightline*. The study's findings left us wondering how other television news programs might compare to *Nightline* in terms of the diversity and inclusiveness of their guest lists.

In response to such questions, we conducted this comparative analysis of the guest lists of ABC's *Nightline* and PBS's *MacNeil/Lehrer NewsHour* for a six month period (2/6/89 to 8/4/89), beginning on the day the first *Nightline* study was released. We chose *MacNeil/Lehrer* for comparison because it seemed to be the only serious challenger to *Nightline* as today's pre-eminent daily news/public affairs program. Also, like *Nightline*, *MacNeil/Lehrer* relies heavily on invited guests to provide analysis and commentary.

Despite the fact that *MacNeil/Lehrer* is the nightly news show of the Public Broadcasting Service, we found that, in most respects, its guest list represented an even narrower segment of the political spectrum than *Nightline*'s.

In addition to comparing *MacNeil/Lehrer* with *Nightline*, we compared the *Nightline* guest list before and after the release of our first study to check for any changes. Since *Nightline* host Ted Koppel and then-executive producer Richard Kaplan publicly concurred with some of our original criticisms, we hoped to find improvement in the diversity of *Nightline*'s guests. Our hopes for significant changes were not met. These findings are reported in the "*Nightline* Follow-Up" section at the end of this chapter.

The *Nightline* Study

Our original study was an examination of the guest list for all of *Nightline*'s 865 programs over a forty month period (1/1/85 to 4/30/88). We argued that *Nightline*'s "in-depth" format, rather than encouraging comprehensive and inclusive reporting, served primarily as a vehicle for the dissemination of the views of a narrow sector of the political spectrum.

The primary criticism levelled against our study was that we were unfairly blaming programs like *Nightline* for simply reflecting the inequities of the "real" world. If certain political views are over-represented, or if men dominate the guest list, it is because these are the characteristics of those in power. However, *Nightline* and similar programs do not just present the views of those in power, they actively solicit the analysis and commentary of non-office holders. Most of *Nightline*'s "regulars" in our original study were not current office-holders; they were largely academics or former officials. Thus *Nightline*'s narrow guest list is not just a reflection of a conservative administration's "decision makers." Instead the boundaries of these guest lists are actively constructed by *Nightline*'s staff and that of other news programs.

We suggest that the news media do not merely reflect some objective reality "out there" in the "real" world. Instead, news is the result of a process in which media personnel make decisions about what is important and what is not, about who is important and who is not, about what views are to be included and what views can be dismissed. None of these decisions can be totally "objective." Instead, widely-shared assumptions underlie the approach media professionals take in making such decisions - assumptions which apply to both *MacNeil/Lehrer* and *Nightline*.

• *"News" is understood to be what those in power say and do.* Broadcast time is largely devoted to the happenings in Washington, D.C. As a result, these programs don't reflect anything close to the available range of views on a particular issue.

• *By limiting the boundaries of acceptable views, the news media legitimize positions and certify "expert" spokespersons while dismissing other positions and labelling their advocates as "parti-*

sans." Advocates of conservative foreign and domestic policy are frequently introduced as reliable "experts"—people whose knowledge results from experience or training. Guests with critical or alternative views, when they do make appearances, are often identified as partisans, with the implication that they are "pursuing an agenda."

• *The limited range of views presented on these programs suggests foreign policy "taboos."* Critical perspectives—those of public interest representatives or progressive academics—do appear occasionally on discussions of domestic political issues, but similar voices are almost never heard in foreign policy debates. Viewers are not offered wide-ranging debate between foreign policy makers and policy critics, whether concerning Central America, Southeast Asia or the Middle East. Substantive discussions about the ends and means of U.S. foreign policy, common in Western European mass media, are simply not available here.

MacNeil/Lehrer's Charlayne Hunter-Gault has commented that "as good and insightful as [network] correspondents are, they must function inside that straightjacket of 22 minutes of nightly news that touches, on average, some 20-odd subjects. That leaves little or no time for context or perspective."[1] *MacNeil/Lehrer* and *Nightline*, on the other hand, purport to offer "context" and "perspective." But which "context and whose "perspective" are featured? This is what we continue to examine in this study.

MacNeil/Lehrer: An Alternative Form Of News?

Because ABC's *Nightline* does not try to survey the range of happenings on a particular day, it is more of a late-night supplement to the nightly news. PBS's *MacNeil/Lehrer NewsHour*, on the other hand, attempts to provide a full-fledged early-evening alternative to the network news. The one-hour program includes a brief "news round-up" of the day's major events followed by a more detailed look at usually three stories.

Several features make *MacNeil/Lehrer* ostensibly different from network programs like *Nightline* or the evening news. In preparing this study, we hypothesized that these characteristics might allow *MacNeil/Lehrer* to provide more inclusive and comprehensive coverage.

First, we thought that the program's airing on the Public Broadcasting Service—with its different financing and different aims from the networks—might have implications for how it approaches the news. The Carnegie Commission Report, from which the Public Broadcasting Act of 1967 was derived, suggested that public television "should be a forum for debate and controversy" and called for public television to "provide a voice for groups in the community that may otherwise be unheard" and to "help us see America whole, in all its diversity."[2] We hoped, therefore, that *MacNeil/Lehrer* would be more concerned with the interest of the public at large rather than with the narrow elites that populate other public affairs programs.

Second, *MacNeil/Lehrer*'s one-hour format is unique among national evening news programs. The program's focus on a limited number of major stories each night means that correspondents sometimes have as much as 10 minutes for their taped reports— almost half of an entire network evening news broadcast. But the bulk of air time is usually devoted to interviews with the program's guest panelists, often its primary sources of information. We thought that the program's lengthy segments might allow for the inclusion of a broader spectrum of views.

Third, *MacNeil/Lehrer* eschews the typical "flashy" network approach in favor of a more conservative appearance and genteel style. (Robert MacNeil's' first book, *The People Machine*, criticized the networks for their sensationalism and consequent distortion of the news.[3]) One PBS insider described *MacNeil/Lehrer* as "the best radio show on television."[4]

The program harks back to an earlier day of "gentlemen's" debates with Robert MacNeil pursuing what he calls "civil interviewing."[5] The program thus makes grayness a virtue and presents a distinctive brand of unimpassioned journalism.

But as we explain below, these differences in format had virtually no positive effect on the inclusiveness and diversity of the *MacNeil/Lehrer* guest list.

Table 4.1

Repeat and Frequent U.S. Guests*
(2/6/89 - 8/4/89)

Nightline Repeat Guests (Two or More Appearances)

Robert Bork	Former Supreme Court nominee
Patrick Buchanan	Former White House Communications Director
Newt Gingrich	U.S. Representative (R-Georgia)
William Gray	U.S. Representative (D-Pennsylvania)
Dennis Kelso	Alaska Environmental Commission
Michael Oksenberg	University of Michigan
Dr. Arnold Relman	*New England Journal of Medicine*
Orville Schell	Author
Alan Simpson	Senator (R-Wyoming)
Nina Totenberg	National Public Radio
Faye Wattleton	Planned Parenthood
Vin Weber	U.S. Representative (R-Minnesota)
Pete Wilson	Senator (R-California)

MacNeil/Lehrer Frequent Guests (Three or More Appearances)

Ed Baumeister	*Trenton Times*
David Bonior	U.S. Representative (D-Michigan)
Richard Cheney	Secretary of Defense
Lee Cullum	*Dallas Times-Herald*
Christopher Dodd	Senator (D-Connecticut)
Mickey Edwards	U.S. Representative (R-Oklahoma)
Thomas Foley	U.S. Representative (D-Washington)
Orrin Hatch	Senator (R-Utah)
Henry Hyde	U.S. Representative (R-Illinois)
William Hyland	*Foreign Affairs*
Kenneth Liebenthal	University of Michigan
Richard Luger	Senator (R-Indiana)
Eleanor Holmes Norton	Georgetown University
Norman Ornstein	American Enterprise Institute
Clarence Page	*Chicago Tribune*
Nina Totenberg	National Public Radio
Malcom Wallop	Senator (R-Wyoming)
Gerald Warren	*San Diego Union*
Fred Wertheimer	Common Cause

*Titles used here are for identification purposes only.

Six-Month Summary

During the six month period we studied, as Table 4.1 shows, 19 guests appeared more than twice on *MacNeil/Lehrer*, and 13 U.S. guests appeared more than once on *Nightline*.

Nightline's repeat guests include five current U.S. government officials, four "experts," and two journalists. *MacNeil/Lehrer*'s frequent guests include nine U.S. government officials, four "experts," and five journalists. Four of *Nightline*'s five government officials (Gingrich, Simpson, Weber and Wilson) were conservatives, while only William Gray can be considered a liberal. Six of *MacNeil/Lehrer*'s nine frequent government officials were conservatives (Cheney, Edwards, Hatch, Hyde, Lugar and Wallop), while only David Bonior and Christopher Dodd can be considered liberals. Despite the Democratic-majority in Congress, most of the repeat lawmakers were Republicans.

Both programs rely heavily on analysts who are not currently government officials or "decision makers"—primarily journalists and "experts". *MacNeil/Lehrer*'s four "experts" include two establishment insiders—Norman Ornstein from the conservative American Enterprise Institute, and William Hyland from the right-tilting journal, *Foreign Affairs*—while Eleanor Holmes Norton was the one "expert" with progressive views. Two of *Nightline*'s four "experts" were right-wing activists (Bork and Buchanan), though not identified as partisans. There were no partisans-as-experts with left-wing perspectives.

Fred Wertheimer of Common Cause was a frequent guest on *MacNeil/Lehrer*, and Faye Wattleton of Planned Parenthood was a repeat guest on *Nightline*. Both were identified as partisans rather than independent "experts." Perhaps this is the most candid way to identify Wertheimer and Wattleton, both of whom represented public interest organizations. Yet the same standard was not applied to conservative partisans, especially those who are former government officials. Pat Buchanan, Robert Bork, William Hyland and Elliott Abrams all may have the credentials of former government officials, but they are also partisans with conservative agendas, not neutral "experts."

For example, when a representative of CISPES (Committee In Solidarity with the People of El Salvador) and Elliott Abrams appeared on *Nightline* to discuss the Salvadoran election (3/17/89), Abrams, then out of government, was identified by his State Department credentials, while CISPES was identified as an organization "supporting the Salvadoran rebels." Similarly, it is misleading to identify Robert Bork as a "scholar in legal studies" (*Nightline*, 7/3/89) without indicating his longstanding association with conservative legal pursuits. In short, many of these "experts" are advocates who should be identified as such.

Since a six-month sample only yields a few repeat guests, looking at the institutional affiliation of guests reveals patterns that an examination of individual guests cannot. On *MacNeil/Lehrer*, two conservative Washington think tanks were featured overwhelmingly: the American Enterprise Institution (AEI) and the Center for Strategic and International Studies (CSIS). AEI fellows appeared six times and CSIS fellows appeared eight times in this six-month period. In simplified terms, AEI provided the resident experts for domestic political issues, and CSIS provided the resident experts for foreign policy issues.

While AEI and CSIS fellows were introduced as nonpartisan "experts," it is clear that both institutes are strong conservative voices. AEI and CSIS receive substantial corporate funding, and both provided many high level appointees to the Reagan Administration.[6] AEI and CSIS fellows should certainly be welcome on *MacNeil/Lehrer*, but why are they not balanced with appearances from progressive think-tanks like the Institute for Policy Studies (IPS) or the World Policy Institute (WPI)? Experts from IPS and WPI did not appear once on *MacNeil/Lehrer* in the six-months we studied.

Nightline did not rely as heavily on these particular think-tanks. AEI fellows appeared only three times and CSIS fellows appeared only once. Still, *Nightline* brings on guests from a variety of other conservative think-tanks and rarely, if ever, invites guests from progressive think-tanks like IPS or WPI. Whenever progressives are featured on *Nightline* they are clearly identified as such, not masked by academic credentials.

Race And Gender

By itself the demographic make-up of these programs' guest lists does not guarantee a diversity of perspectives. However, demo-

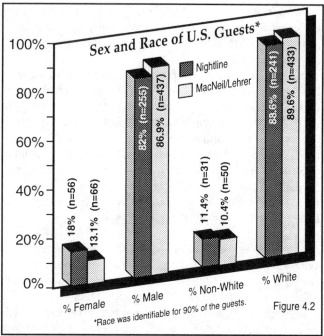

Sex and Race of U.S. Guests*

Nightline
MacNeil/Lehrer

% Female — 18% (n=56), 13.1% (n=66)
% Male — 82% (n=255), 86.9% (n=437)
% Non-White — 11.4% (n=31), 10.4% (n=50)
% White — 88.6% (n=241), 89.6% (n=433)

*Race was identifiable for 90% of the guests.

Figure 4.2

graphic variety is one important sign of substantive diversity. As Figure 4.2 illustrates, both *MacNeil/Lehrer* and *Nightline* had disproportionate numbers of white males on their guest lists. For *MacNeil/Lehrer*, 90 percent of its guests were white and 87 percent were male. *Nightline* was only slightly broader in this regard: 89 percent were white and 82 percent were male.[7]

On programs about international politics the numbers are even more stark: 94 percent of *MacNeil/Lehrer*'s U.S. guests were white and 94 percent were male, while 96 percent of *Nightline*'s U.S. guests were white and 90 percent were male. Thus, during discussions about foreign policy, on which *Nightline*'s reputation is largely based, women and people of color from the U.S. were, for all practical purposes, non-participants.

Coverage of domestic politics was more representative. Twenty-one percent of the U.S. guests on *MacNeil/Lehrer* were women and 26 percent of *Nightline*'s guests were women. A

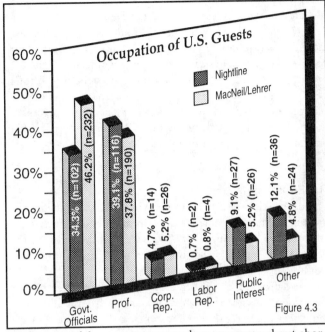

Figure 4.3

good many of the women appeared on programs about abortion, where debates were generally inclusive. All three *Nightline* programs about abortion featured activists on both sides of the debate.

Occupation

MacNeil/Lehrer relies heavily on current and former government officials. Figure 4.3 shows that a total of 46 percent of *MacNeil/Lehrer*'s U.S. guests were current or former government officials. Another 38 percent were professionals (primarily academics, doctors, and lawyers) and 5 percent were corporate representatives. A total of 89 percent of *MacNeil/Lehrer*'s U.S. guests represent elite opinion, while only 6 percent represent public interest, labor or racial/ethnic organizations. On programs about international politics, 67 percent of *MacNeil/Lehrer*'s U.S. guests were current or former government officials. It is not surprising, then, that *MacNeil/Lehrer*'s "debates" are usually less-than provocative.

Nightline also relies heavily on similar elites, but it shows more diversity in its guest list than *MacNeil/Lehrer*. Thirty-four percent of the U.S. guests were government officials, 39 percent professionals, and 5 percent corporate representatives. A total of 78 percent of the guests represent elite opinion, while 10 percent represent public interest, labor or racial/ethnic organizations. While this is clearly broader than *MacNeil/Lehrer*, it is still far from a diverse sample of opinion.

Case Studies
The Environment

The destruction of our natural environment is arguably the most significant issue facing humanity at the end of the twentieth century. Ted Koppel (3/7/89) has called the threat to the ozone layer "perhaps the most imminent danger now confronting this planet."

In a program on the ozone layer, Koppel commented that "what we are doing to ourselves may have such devastating consequences that we will wonder some day how we could have been distracted by such trivial concerns as earthquakes, or famine, or flood." Yet in the same program Koppel seemed to offer his own answer. He said, "Politically this is not an exciting issue. In fact, it causes people's eyes to glaze over when you start talking about some of these issues."

After decades of ignoring warnings from environmental activists and scientists, the mainstream media are finally beginning to pay more attention to growing ecological devastation. Despite this trend, the environment still poses two major difficulties for the news media. First, the environment is rarely a "breaking" story. The dangers and developments affecting the environment evolve gradually over a period of time. There is not always a convenient "peg" on which to hang an environmental story. The exception proves the rule: the dramatic Exxon oil spill in Alaska provided journalists with a compelling story and powerful visuals. Nearly half of the environmental stories during our study focused on this spill.

Second, environmentalists know that in order to fully assess the issue of ecological destruction one has to "follow the money." For journalists this can pose problems. Tracing environmental damage back to the corporate and industrial organizations which benefit from weak environmental protection laws might result in pressure from corporate advertisers or underwriters. Even when environmental stories are covered, the role of corporate polluters is often obscured. As Ralph Nader has noted, "Look at all the stories on the destruction of the Amazon rain forest. Do you ever see the names of any multinational corporations mentioned?"[8] *MacNeil/Lehrer*'s July 4, 1989 story on Brazil's Amazon rain forest was no exception; no corporations were mentioned.

MacNeil/Lehrer featured 16 environment-related stories. Besides the Exxon Valdez spill, subjects included President Bush's "clean air" proposals, other oil spills, environmental/safety problems at nuclear weapons facilities, the search for nuclear waste sites, driftnet fishing, the food additive Alar, Brazil's rain forest and a proposed dam outside Denver.

A total of 17 guests, all white American males, appeared on *MacNeil/Lehrer*'s environmental segments. If viewers expected to find representatives from environmental groups on programs about the environment, they were disappointed. Only one representative of an environmental organization appeared. Instead, government and corporate representatives dominated *MacNeil/Lehrer*'s guest list for environmental stories. More than half of the guests were government officials, while almost one-third were corporate representatives.

MacNeil/Lehrer's inattention to environmentalists is highlighted by the sole case in which an environmentalist actually made an appearance. On March 16, 1989, Al Meyeroff of the Natural Resources Defense Council was on *MacNeil/Lehrer* to discuss NRDC's report on the dangers of Alar, the food additive. Since NRDC was the source of the Alar story, it would have been virtually impossible for *MacNeil/Lehrer* to cover it without including an NRDC representative. Such was not the case for most environmental stories and no other environmentalists were guests on the show.

When *MacNeil/Lehrer* discussed the government's plan to clean up environmental and safety problems at major nuclear weapons plants (8/2/89), it invited Energy Secretary James Watkins for a "Newsmaker" interview—alone with no dissenting guests. When *MacNeil/Lehrer* examined President Bush's proposals for cleaner air (6/12/89), it invited the Environmental Protection Agency's (EPA) William Reilly—alone with no dissenting guests.

Without critical voices, many of *MacNeil/Lehrer*'s environmental programs presented extremely limited perspectives, sometimes with corporate and government voices supporting each other. *MacNeil/Lehrer* featured the Alaska oil spill on four consecutive programs, and had three later follow-ups. The first program featured Exxon's Alaska Coordinator, Don Cornett,

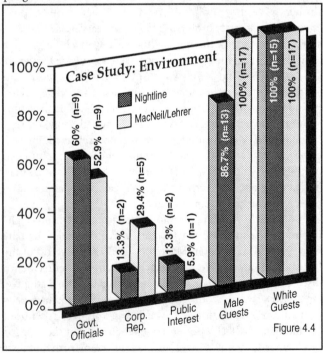

Figure 4.4

and Alaskan Governor Steve Cowper. Cornett assured the audience (wrongly, it turns out) that, with chemical dispersants, Exxon would "handle a great deal of the spill before it ever touches the shore line of Prince William Sound" and argues that "people tend to forget that oil is biodegradable." For his part, Governor Cowper expressed concern at the lack of preparedness by the oil company, but felt that this spill should not interfere with future expansion of oil drilling in the Arctic. He concluded, "By and large the Trans Alaska Pipeline is a very effective way to get oil from one place to another. It's clean from an engineering standpoint and while there have been some relatively minor incidents, I think that they're acceptable." No environmentalists were present to challenge such declarations.

While the scale of the spill could not be overlooked, government experts and corporate representatives presented a largely reassuring view of the impact of the accident. Exxon chairman Lawrence Rawl was featured on the fourth story *MacNeil/Lehrer* did on the spill (3/30/89). He apologized for the spill, but downplayed its impact on the oil industry. Rawl's appearance was "balanced" by Governor Cowper who, while criticizing the oil company consortium responsible for clean-up plans, argued that "the chairman of the board of Exxon, I think, has been too heavy on his own company…. Obviously Exxon's skipper caused this accident but after it took place, I think that Exxon did a good job under the circumstances. I really do."

Nightline featured environmental issues on only six out of 130 programs, with a total of 15 guests. All the guests were white and only two were women. All but one guest (Margaret Thatcher) were U.S. citizens. A full 60 percent of the guests were government officials while 13 percent were corporate representatives. *Nightline* included only two environmentalists—Wilderness Society president George Frampton (on the future of oil spills) and Janet Hathaway of the National Resources Defense Council (health effects of pesticides.)

The Exxon oil spill dominated *Nightline*'s coverage of the environment. *Nightline's* three programs on the spill, spread over a four-month period, had a decidedly more skeptical tone than *MacNeil/Lehrer*'s. Its first program featured a spokesperson for the Alaska Department of Environmental Conservation, the agency conducting on-site coordination of the oil spill cleanup; the mayor of Valdez; and a fisherman, Jim Brown. The inclusion of Brown was a rare case where the perspectives of someone affected by events was included. It's worth noting that Exxon, which had sent a representative to appear on *MacNeil/Lehrer* on the same day, turned down *Nightline*'s invitation to have a spokesperson on the program. (The same thing occurred on July 25 when Exxon turned down a *Nightline* invitation to appear, but sent Exxon president Lee Raymond to appear on *MacNeil/Lehrer* two days later.)

While Koppel did ask tougher questions about the bungled clean-up operations, the programs relied heavily on government and corporate experts for commentary and analysis. For example, Dennis Kelso from the Alaska Environmental Commission was on all three of *Nightline*'s Alaskan oil spill programs. In a taped introduction to one program, ABC's Roger Caras said: "The torn hull of the Exxon Valdez is the greatest environmental 'I told you so' in history." Yet notably absent from any of the Exxon oil spill programs were representatives from environmental groups that had long warned about such an incident.

What *Nightline* and *MacNeil/Lehrer*'s environmental coverage reveals is a good deal of lip service to the importance of environmental issues with an apparent lack of commitment to serious ongoing coverage. Even more disturbing is a disregard for the views of environmentalists, the very people who have long struggled to bring attention to the plight of the earth's environment.

There are a wide variety of respected environmental organizations in the United States—Sierra Club, Greenpeace, Earth Island Institute, League of Conservation Voters, National Toxics Campaign, among others—with well-informed representatives who could be valuable assets in illuminating the admittedly complex issues associated with environmental destruction. *MacNeil/Lehrer* and *Nightline* should be calling upon them much more frequently.

The Economy

Perhaps the most striking feature of *MacNeil/Lehrer* and *Nightline*'s economic coverage is its narrow focus. News programs focus more on Washington budget debates than on economic trends in particular industries or in the nation's labor force. Consequently much of the "economic" reporting on television is really about Washington political debates. In this section, we limit ourselves to programs which actually discussed economic issues, whether in particular industries, the U.S. as a whole, or the world. For *MacNeil/Lehrer*, and even more so for *Nightline*, such economic coverage is scant.

MacNeil/Lehrer aired 35 segments on economic issues with a total of 42 guests. Only four of the 42 guests were women; two appeared on a program about the "mommy track"—the separate corporate career track for women who plan to have children. Economic coverage on *MacNeil/Lehrer* was characterized by a heavy reliance on government spokespersons. Government officials made up 41 percent of the guests, while corporate representatives accounted for another 29 percent and professionals 21 percent. Only 10 percent were labor representatives.

The most heavily covered economic issue during our study was the Eastern airline strike and subsequent bankruptcy of the airline. *MacNeil/Lehrer* aired five stories on this topic. It was during this coverage that all four appearances by labor leaders took place. The strike provided for a dramatic conflict with two clearly demarcated sides: union and management. *MacNeil/Lehrer* did a good job at soliciting the union's opinions to balance those of Eastern airline executives.

Unfortunately, this was the only time that the views of workers or their representatives were ever considered in *MacNeil/Lehrer*'s economic coverage. No labor or consumer rights representatives appeared on *MacNeil/Lehrer*'s other 14 economic stories that featured guests. When the program did a story on the U.S. government's suit to seize control of the Teamsters union, no union or rank & file representatives were on the show. Instead, the only guest was a reporter from the Long

Island newspaper *Newsday*. A week-long series on the "Hi-Tech Frontier" did not have any labor or consumer representatives as guests.

Watching *MacNeil/Lehrer*, a viewer might think that workers are not part of the economic realm. Instead, government

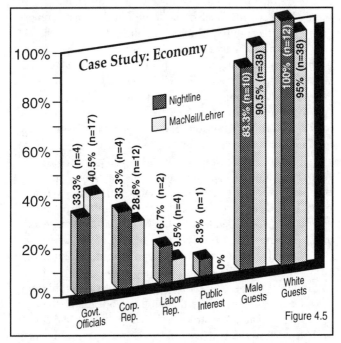

Figure 4.5

officials, corporate representatives and professional "experts" populate *MacNeil/Lehrer*'s economic reports. The budget deficit and the Savings and Loan bailout did not include any consumer rights advocates. The economic conditions of workers who make up the vast majority of our economy are rarely considered. For example, the Pittston coal strike which began in April and lasted through the end of our study was never featured on either *MacNeil/Lehrer* or *Nightline*.

Nightline ran four programs with a total of 12 guests on economic issues. Only two women appeared; both were on a program about the "mommy track." One-third of the guests were government officials and one-third were corporate representatives. Seventeen percent were labor representatives. Professionals and public interest representatives each had one guest (8 percent). Despite its usual attention to international events, all of *Nightline*'s economic stories were focused on the United States.

Nightline's four economic programs were on the indictment of junk bond king Michael Milken, the damage to United Flight 811 and airline industry's aging aircraft, the debate over Felice Schwartz's article on the "mommy track," and the bankruptcy of Eastern airlines. Prompted by dramatic, individual events, these are the kind of stories covered on the evening news.

Typically missing from *MacNeil/Lehrer* and *Nightline* was analytical coverage of economic trends. The one exception was *MacNeil/Lehrer*'s series on the "High-Tech Frontier" which attempted to analyze an issue which did not easily lend itself to short news formats.

Also generally missing from both programs' economic coverage were women, people of color, consumer rights advocates, and labor representatives. Just as the media tend to equate the nation with the federal government, they also equate the "economy" with corporate management and government officials, to the exclusion of the workers and consumers who make up the bulk of the economy.

China

The student-led occupation of Tiananmen Square was the major story of the summer of 1989, and both *MacNeil/Lehrer* and *Nightline* gave it a great deal of air time. Both programs did an impressive job of keeping abreast of events, with daily updates on breaking news. But analysis of the history, motivations and consequences of the student movement and the government response were severely limited.

MacNeil/Lehrer ran 18 segments that focused on China during our study, with a total of 37 guests. Seventy-three percent of these guests were from the US, while the remainder were from China. In total, 61 percent of the guests were white, while 39 percent were Asian, showing *MacNeil/Lehrer*'s inclusion of both Chinese citizens and Chinese-Americans. Eighty-nine percent of the guests were men, despite the fact that the news media were heralding the important leadership role played by female students in China.

The occupational breakdown of the guest list was broader than for other international issues. Thirty percent of the guests were government officials, 46 percent professionals (mainly academics and journalists), and 14 percent were public interest activists. These activists were all Chinese students either living in the U.S. during the hostilities or fleeing to the U.S. shortly after. The most frequent guest was Pei Minxin, a Chinese student attending Harvard. Pei made five appearances on *MacNeil/Lehrer*, representing one perspective amongst the diverse student activists. *MacNeil/Lehrer* never made clear exactly who Pei is, or why he was chosen to speak on behalf of the students; his appearances suggested he had access to information from inside the Chinese student movement.

Nightline's coverage was even more extensive than *MacNeil/Lehrer*'s: China was *Nightline*'s story 10 nights in a row in early June. During the period we studied, there were 19 China programs with 49 guests. Fifty-three percent of the guests were from the US, while the remainder included foreign journalists, Chinese dissidents, and Chinese student activists. Fifty-one percent of the guests were white, while 49 percent were were Asians or Asian-Americans.

Nightline's coverage of China was significantly different than its coverage of other international issues as only one-tenth of the guests were government officials, while 20 percent were public interest activists. This is the only issue in our study in which activists outnumber government officials. The activists were all Chinese student leaders, and, as with *MacNeil/Lehrer*, Pei Minxin was the most frequent guest, appearing four times, including three consecutive nights. It was refreshing to see *Nightline* pay so much attention to "unofficial" views of events. Were *Nightline* to seek out "unofficial" sources on a variety of other topics, its coverage might improve a great deal.

MacNeil/Lehrer and *Nightline* covered the story in China much as TV news covers natural disasters, with a premium on getting the latest information, reporting the casualties, and providing video footage. But *MacNeil/Lehrer* and *Nightline* are

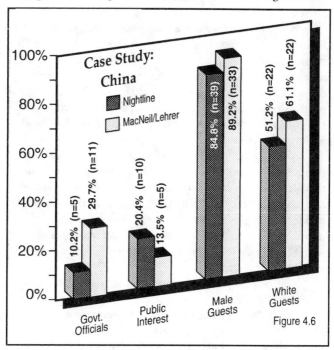

Figure 4.6

capable of providing more than just the drama of the nightly news. These programs purport to offer in-depth analysis of events. Yet they failed to seriously examine the history leading up to the 1989 student activism, the reasons for unrest, and the demands of the students.

Perhaps it was not surprising that *Nightline* failed to discuss China's recent history more thoroughly; it only broadcast one program on China between 1985 and 1988, a time when a student movement was repressed and the human rights situation was dire. Setbacks to democracy in China during the mid-

80's were ignored by most U.S. media, which were content to hail China's openness to Western investment.[9] The media's disinterest in China's human rights situation was shared by the U.S. government—as China was becoming an increasingly important U.S. ally in regional conflicts in Asia, Southern Africa and Central America.

When the media asserted that the Chinese students were leading a "pro-democracy" movement, they rarely explored the meaning of this label. It was as if "pro-democracy" was somehow self-explanatory. The student movement grew, in part, in response to the problems of free market experiments. Popular protest slogans were "Eradicate privilege" and "Down with official racketeering." Yet *MacNeil/Lehrer* and *Nightline* failed to explore these issues.

Nightline made no effort to connect discussions of corruption to economic "reforms"—which, when they were mentioned, were heralded uncritically. Nor did viewers learn what the pro-democracy students thought of socialism as an economic system. Were they calling for a US-style political and economic system? Also absent from the programs' coverage was serious attention to the reasons why many workers decided to support student efforts.

The "mirror" these programs held up to the world excluded significant historical roots of the protests. For example, the mid-1980's student movement in China was mentioned on only four of the 19 Nightline programs, each time only in passing. There was so little historical context that on May 28 Koppel described the movement as one that had emerged "so suddenly." Without any information about recent Chinese history, viewers of *Nightline* would be almost certain to concur.

Central America

Seven *MacNeil/Lehrer* programs featured segments on Central America: two on the Salvadoran election, two on aid to the Nicaraguan contras, and three on the Panamanian election. All

22 of the guests were men and all of the U.S. guests were white. Perhaps most interesting is the fact that 100 percent of the guests were current or former government officials from the U.S. or elsewhere. Furthermore, all of the foreign government officials were friendly to the US—there were no voices from the Nicaraguan government.

MacNeil/Lehrer's coverage of Central America presented essentially one side of this multifaceted issue, without even an attempt at pluralism. Democrats and Republicans may disagree on the tactics of U.S. policy, but they rarely disagree on the "democratic" goals of that policy or on the "good" intentions of the U.S. government. And friendly foreign government officials seeking U.S. support are not likely to fundamentally disagree with U.S. officials.

What makes this kind of coverage curious is that the U.S. government's (often bipartisan) policies towards Central America have been vigorously condemned by a significant part of the world community, and by large sectors of the U.S. population, especially in academia, the religious community, and the labor movement. Yet as far as MacNeil/Lehrer is concerned, these critical perspectives do not exist; the only views that matter are those of the U.S. government.

MacNeil/Lehrer's coverage of Nicaragua and the contras featured appearances by two U.S. congressmen, Secretary of State James Baker, and Guatemalan President Vinicio Cerezo. The discussion did not include any voices from Nicaragua, nor did it include any leaders of the anti-intervention movement in the US. There was such a consensual atmosphere on MacNeil/Lehrer that one would never have known that polls indicated that a majority of the U.S. population had opposed U.S. policy toward Nicaragua for years.

The choice of Guatemalan President Cerezo to discuss human rights abuses and democratic shortcomings in Nicaragua was quite telling, since Cerezo's US-backed government stood accused by human rights monitors of involvement in the disappearances and abductions of dozens of Guatemalan civilians each month. The findings of independent human rights groups indicate that the human rights situation in Guatemala was significantly worse than in Nicaragua. While the selection of Cerezo to judge Nicaragua tended to distort human rights realities in the region, it conformed perfectly with U.S. government propaganda contrasting Guatemala's "burgeoning democ-

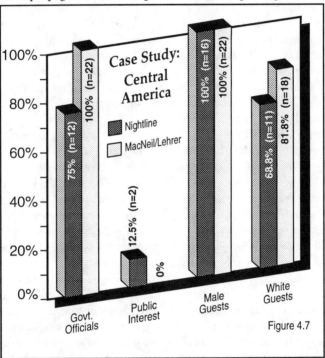

Case Study: Central America

Nightline
MacNeil/Lehrer

Figure 4.7

racy" with "repressive" Nicaragua. Robert MacNeil also adhered to U.S. propaganda when he opened his interview with Cerezo by charging that the Sandinistas made and broke promises about having free elections in the past. MacNeil did not refer to any specifics and he neglected to mention the 1984 elections in Nicaragua which were certified as free and fair by neutral international observers.

MacNeil/Lehrer's coverage of El Salvador focused on the March 1989 election in which Alfredo Cristiani of the ARENA

party was elected. The guests were two U.S. congressmen prais-
ing the election, as well as a "Newsmaker" interview with
President-elect Cristiani. Again, no opposition voices from the
U.S. were heard—even at a time when there was widespread
opposition to Washington's support of the Salvadoran government. Furthermore, there were no voices of the armed FMLN
opposition in El Salvador, or of recently-returned opposition
politicians who had risked their lives to participate in the elections. In sum, *MacNeil/Lehrer*'s coverage of Central America
was so one-sided that it provided viewers with little substance at
all.

Nightline*'s coverage of Central America, while more inclusive than *MacNeil/Lehrer*'s, had some of the same shortcomings.
Nightline broadcast six programs featuring discussion of Central
America: two on the Salvadoran elections and four about the
Panamanian election. All 16 of the guests were men and all of
the U.S. guests were white. Three-quarters of the guests were
current or former government officials.

However, *Nightline*'s few guests who were not government
officials made a large difference. *Nightline*'s coverage of the
Salvadoran election was generally commendable. Each of its two
programs—on the eve of the election and the day after the election— presented diverse views. On the eve of the election
Nightline hosted a debate between Elliott Abrams, former architect of the Reagan policy in Central America, and Michael Lent
of CISPES, a national organization which opposes U.S. policy
and supports the Salvadoran opposition. This configuration of
guests made for a more substantive debate than the traditional
discussions limited to Democratic and Republican leadership;
Abrams and Lent—both passionate partisans, although only
Lent was clearly identified as such—were able to argue fundamental issues about politics in El Salvador and in the US.

The day after the election *Nightline* hosted the president-
elect, Cristiani, along with one of the highest ranking members of
the political opposition in El Salvador, Ruben Zamora. Unlike
MacNeil/Lehrer, which interviewed Cristiani alone, *Nightline*
brought Cristiani on to debate a political opponent, leading to a

more informative program.

Nightline's coverage of the Panamanian elections also included more perspectives than MacNeil/Lehrer's coverage. Seventy percent of the guests on Nightline's programs about Panama were U.S. officials. The others included both pro- and anti-Noriega forces. Still, no U.S. policy critics appeared as guests. Nor was there substantive discussion about the past relationship between the U.S. and Noriega.

Terrorism

MacNeil/Lehrer and Nightline had remarkably similar coverage of terrorism in the period covered by this study. Both featured six programs on terrorism—the bulk of which were about the "hostage crisis" triggered by the killing of Colonel Higgins, the Beirut hostage.

On MacNeil/Lehrer, 70 percent of the guests were current or former government officials. Ninety-five percent of the guests were white and over 90 percent were men. There were no voices from a critical or alternative perspective. Instead of a spectrum of opinions debating U.S. policy, it was a procession of the same "experts" who always appear on discussions of terrorism: Brian Jenkins of the Rand Corporation; Neil Livingstone of the Institute on Terrorism and Subnational Conflict; former U.S. government counterterrorism "experts" Noel Koch and L. Paul Bremer; and Edward Luttwak of CSIS. These men rarely disagree. They all agree, for example, on the importance of reserving the right to "retaliate" militarily, and stress the importance of "counterterrorism." Nowhere in the discussion was there any real questioning of the underpinning of U.S. policies toward terrorism or the Middle East; and nowhere was the military option debated with any seriousness.

Nightline's coverage of terrorism was little different. Two of the terrorism programs focused on the hostages in Lebanon, two on airport security, one on the political problems hostages present to U.S. presidents, and one looked at the Chilean fruit scare as a terrorist activity. While Nightline may have defined a marginally broader range of issues as terrorism (MacNeil/Lehrer covered the Chilean fruit scare as a public health issue, not a terrorist issue), its range of viewpoints was little different from *MacNeil/Lehrer*'s. Seventy-four percent of the guests were current or former government officials and, as with *MacNeil/Lehrer*, no alternative voices were aired.

Nightline relied less on terrorist "experts" than *MacNeil/Lehrer*, as Brian Jenkins of the Rand Corporation was the only guest of this type. Instead, *Nightline* enlisted a series of former U.S. government officials and current Israeli officials to discuss terrorism. Israel's Ehud Olmert and Benjamin Netanyahu both appeared on *Nightline* to discuss the hostage situation. Perhaps their expertise was sought due to their central role in the ongoing crisis. Yet there are a variety of opinions in Israel—both inside and outside the government—and Olmert and Netanyahu represent a distinctly hardline perspective. It is similar to the perspective shared by the former U.S.

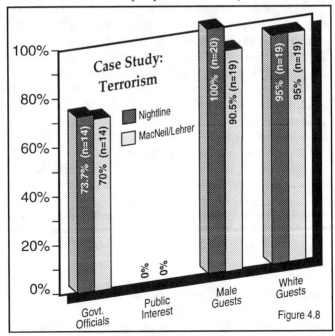

Figure 4.8

officials *Nightline* presented: Patrick Buchanan, Henry Kissinger, and Bobby Inman. In fact, Buchanan was the only repeat guest in *Nightline*'s set of six terrorism programs. It is unclear, aside from tough rhetoric, what makes Buchanan an expert on terrorism.

As with *MacNeil/Lehrer*, no underlying issues were examined on *Nightline*'s discussions of terrorism. The focus was generally on the use of U.S. military force. Rather than debating U.S. policy, Ted Koppel handed his August 3 program over to Henry Kissinger to run a simulated National Security Council meeting with five other former government officials, including Buchanan. Perhaps viewers found this interesting, and Koppel himself said he was "rather amazed at how much substance" emerged in the discussion. But it did not appear to be news or journalism. It seemed more an attempt to outflank the Bush administration on its right wing, encouraging a military approach.

The problem with *MacNeil/Lehrer* and *Nightline*'s coverage of terrorism is that there is no substantive debate—who commits terrorism, how it can be stopped, what are its roots. Instead it is framed as a technical, not a political problem, one that "experts" can solve. Guests with the same assumptions so dominate both programs that no policy questions were ever challenged. Never was the discussion linked to a broader discussion of political violence. Nor did they ever discuss what differentiates counterterrorism, if anything, from terrorism.

Several U.S. administrations have faced terrorism crises, yet little progress has been made. Television news has been content to trot out the same commentators and experts to make all the same points. Perhaps 10 years of this has made it seem as if there are no other views on terrorism. If programs like *MacNeil/Lehrer* and *Nightline* would seek out and present alternative perspectives, perhaps the U.S. public would benefit from some new thinking on the subject.

Unrealized Potential and the Beltway Mentality

Extended news programs offer the potential for significantly expanding the boundaries of television journalism. Their format is conducive to more in-depth coverage than the half-hour evening news. The *MacNeil/Lehrer NewsHour*, in particular, is uniquely positioned to present more systematic coverage of issues which are not neatly "pegged" to a daily event and which cannot be easily summarized in a brief evening news report. On occasion, it has successfully done so.

One example was the ongoing series, "Talking Drugs," which tried to explore the day-to-day realities of drug use and abuse and some of the complex economic, social, and political issues involved - albeit with a focus on punishment and rehabilitation rather than the causes of drug abuse. While the series sometimes relied on the usual academics and government officials, it included interviews with people who are normally excluded from the usual government/expert guest list. Charlayne Hunter-Gault, who hosted the series, talked with a former drug abuser turned drug counselor, with a former drug addict who went through a residential recovery program, and a former San Francisco drug dealer who now works against drug abuse in the city's African-American community. By asking these sources to evaluate the government's "war on drugs" and suggest alternatives to it, the series presented a range of perspectives on an issue which has been saturated with redundant coverage from other news outlets.

Unfortunately, "Talking Drugs" is a rare exception. By and large the promise of broad, in-depth coverage on *MacNeil/Lehrer* remains unfulfilled. Instead, *MacNeil/Lehrer*'s guest list represents an extremely narrow segment of the political and social spectrum. The program relies too heavily on official Washington for both story topics and guests. The rise and fall of personalities and the unfolding dramas of Washington's internal political debates fill the program like a national soap opera populated by an elite cast of characters.

What is most striking about *MacNeil/Lehrer*'s coverage of Washington politics is the sheer volume of it. When George Bush proposed John Tower as secretary of defense to a reluctant Congress, *MacNeil/Lehrer* offered 11 stories on the nomination process, including several extended excerpts from the Senate debate. When House Speaker Jim Wright was charged with ethics violations and subsequently resigned, *MacNeil/Lehrer* had 10 different stories on it. Another 10 stories were devoted to the HUD scandal during the period of our study.

When *MacNeil/Lehrer* covered Washington politics, 60 percent of its guests were government officials. In addition, the program's Washington-centeredness was often augmented by lengthy excerpts from congressional hearings, floor debates, and press conferences. When it comes to the inner workings of Washington, *MacNeil/Lehrer* serves as a veritable press agency for the views of U.S. officialdom— one that excludes the views of critics.

Our hypothesis that public television would allow for greater diversity, by removing the pressures of advertising dollars and corporate ownership, proved incorrect. Perhaps these pressures were merely supplanted by those associated with corporate underwriting.

The *NewsHour* evolved from the original *MacNeil/Lehrer Report*, a half-hour program covering a single issue each day. After *Nightline* set the new standard for the half-hour, single-issue program, it was proposed in November 1982 that *MacNeil/Lehrer* expand to a full hour. The proposal was cooly received by many public stations. But the new format had the support of AT&T—to the tune of $10 million, nearly half of the show's $21 million cost.[10]

There are obviously many factors behind *MacNeil/Lehrer*'s narrow guest list. We wonder whether the need to attract corporate underwriters counteracts any freedom achieved through the non-commercial nature of PBS. Or whether the problem stems from the political concerns of *MacNeil/Lehrer*'s decisions-makers. Former staffers have pointed out that co-anchor Jim Lehrer has no interest in the views of public interest representatives, whom Lehrer dismissed as "moaners and whiners."[11]

Compounding the problems caused by the lack of critical guests, the *NewsHour*'s hosts do not play the role of critical interrogators. Few challenging questions are asked. Guests are often left free to answer open-ended questions.

A comparison with *MacNeil/Lehrer* reveals some of

Nightline's strengths and weaknesses. For example, *Nightline* makes use of its budget and technological capabilities to cover events all over the globe. *Nightline* is much more likely than *MacNeil/Lehrer* to include foreign guests. While *Nightline* can be commended for its inclusion of foreign spokespersons, it should be faulted for its inattention to U.S. critics. Like *MacNeil/Lehrer*, it features a narrow team of important "players."

In the end, this study reaffirms the key findings of our first *Nightline* report. Both *MacNeil/Lehrer* and *Nightline* fall far short of being politically or socially inclusive. Their limited political scope generally excludes critics in favor of voices of the powerful. Conservative advocates regularly appear as "experts," while progressives are identified as partisans. And foreign policy debates are almost the exclusive property of policy makers.

Perhaps Ted Koppel and others are correct in arguing that these programs' guest lists merely reflect the characteristics of those in power. Yet a democratic society can not be content with news coverage that acts primarily to transmit the views of the powerful. On the contrary, a healthy democracy needs a media that can present multiple perspectives on issues and events. When the media regularly exclude significant views within the U.S. population—the voices of women, people of color, political minorities, environmentalists and other public interest representatives—it effectively undermines the democratic ideal of a free press.

Nightline Follow-Up

When our first *Nightline* study was released in February 1989, it received a good deal of media attention. While criticizing our report, (see Chapter 6) *Nightline*'s Ted Koppel and then-executive producer Richard Kaplan admitted that *Nightline* sometimes "gets into a rut" and concurred with some of the study's criticisms. Many were curious how *Nightline* would respond to the original study, not in word, but in deed. Beginning February 6, 1989, the day on which the original study was released, we undertook this six-month follow-up study.

Regulars
In the follow-up study, the *Nightline* guest list was not populated so heavily by the "usual suspects." The four most frequent guests from our first study—Kissinger, Haig, Falwell, Abrams—made only two appearances during the six months of our follow-up study (Kissinger and Abrams, once each). Furthermore, while the 19 U.S. guests who were "regulars" during our first study had appeared a total of 159 times in 40 months (3.98 appearances per month), the same 19 men appeared only 10 times in the six months since the study's release (1.67 appearances per month). This represents a 58 percent decrease. Unfortunately, the 13 repeat guests in the current six-month study were little different in type or opinions than the first study's regulars.

Gender
Women, who made up only 11 percent of the U.S. guests in the original study, made up 18 percent of the U.S. guests in the six months following. Few of the female guests appeared on discussions of international politics (90 percent male). There was, however, a significant increase in the participation of women in discussion of domestic issues—up from 11 percent to 26 percent of the guests. Even with more women appearing on the program, female guests still appeared later in the program (they were half as likely as men to appear before the first commercial break) and women spoke, on average, 12 percent less than male guests. Both figures are similar to results from our first study.

Race
There was little change in the area of race: 89 percent of the U.S. guests were white, down from 92 percent in our original study. White guests were twice as likely to appear early in the program as African-American or Latino guests.

Occupation
The percentage of elites—government officials, corporate representatives, professionals—changed little. Elites made up approximately 80 percent of the guest list in both studies. But

the participation of public interest representatives almost doubled—from 6 percent to 10 percent of the U.S. guests. Most of this change occurred on programs about domestic issues where public interest activists made up 12 percent of the U.S. guests. (The increase stemmed partly from abortion programs, which highlighted the views of activists on both sides.) On international issues, the figure remained at 5 percent. Elites were more likely to appear early on the program: 7 percent appeared before the first break, while not one public interest representative did. Government officials spoke on-average 14 percent more than public interest representatives, down from 23 percent more in the first study.

Central America

Our first study suggested weaknesses which Koppel and Kaplan acknowledged. In the six months following, *Nightline*'s Central America coverage was more inclusive, exemplified by the appearance of a representative of CISPES, a U.S. anti-intervention group. Days later, leftist leader Ruben Zamora appeared along with newly elected President Cristiani, another unusually diverse selection of guests. Coverage of Panama during the summer of 1989 had foreign critics of U.S. policy—in particular, Panamanian official Mario Rognoni appeared twice—but there was no real debate between U.S. guests.

In contrast to *Nightline*'s apparent Nicaragua obsession from 1985 to 1988, when it featured 22 programs, no *Nightline* programs in the six month following February 6, 1989 dealt with Nicaragua. While this suggests a greater willingness to deal with the rest of the region, it's worth noting that programs on Guatemala or Honduras were, again, conspicuously absent. Perhaps the real change was in the White House. While the Reagan administration had waged a high profile campaign against Nicaragua, the Bush administration continued similar policy but with a distinctly lower profile. Throughout 1989, there were newsworthy happenings related to Nicaragua, yet *Nightline* chose not to cover them. The dramatic dropoff in Nicaragua coverage suggests the power the White House wields in defining media agendas.

Terrorism

Ted Koppel acknowledged the validity of our criticisms in this area, saying that Nightline had looked at terrorism "much too narrowly" and had not done "as many programs as we ought [to] on state terrorism"[12] Yet we found no change at all. The same people carried on the same discussions. No alternative voices were heard. And there was no broadening of *Nightline*'s definition of terrorism, as it continued to ignore the state terror of an array of US-backed regimes.

There has been some improvement in *Nightline*'s diversity. More critical voices appeared and there was less reliance on the usual suspects. Still, there continues to be an overwhelming reliance on the same types of people—white men from powerful institutions. Foreign policy debates still lack a critical edge, and the inclusion of dissenting voices continues to be the exception.

Postscript: The Kwitny Comparison

How might a more inclusive news program look? To answer this question, we looked at the guest list of *The Kwitny Report*, a weekly PBS program hosted by Jonathan Kwitny, author and former *Wall Street Journal* reporter. Kwitny aired 20 programs during the 1988-1989 season, with a total of 40 guests. It covered many of the same topics as *Nightline* and *MacNeil/Lehrer*: Eastern Europe, U.S. energy policy, Central America, the Philippines.

Although the vast majority of guests were white men, *Kwitny* included a wider range of perspectives than *Nightline* or *MacNeil/Lehrer*. In contrast to the other two programs, *Kwitny* regularly included critical or public interest voices.

Indeed, public interest representatives (33 percent of the total guests) appeared almost as frequently as government officials (35 percent of total.)

On a regular basis, the *Kwitny Report* offered substantive debates which included views of more than just "the usual suspects." For example, a program about nuclear weapons included defense establishment figures McGeorge Bundy and Gen. Daniel Graham, along with critic Daniel Ellsberg. A program on energy policy included a U.S. senator, a corporate representative and an environmentalist. And a program about U.S. foreign aid featured a former U.S. Agency for International Development official along with policy critic Frances Moore Lappe.

The contrast between *Kwitny* and *MacNeil/Lehrer* was demonstrated quite graphically in February 1989, when *MacNeil/Lehrer* presented US-backed Guatemalan President Cerezo as an expert on human rights in Nicaragua. During the same month, *Kwitny* presented two programs with panels that included an Americas Watch expert and a Guatemalan labor leader, examining human rights violations then being committed by the Guatemalan government. No Guatemalan official consented to appear on *Kwitny*, perhaps because, unlike on *MacNeil/Lehrer*, they would have been asked to defend the human rights situation in Guatemala.

The *Kwitny Report* proved that a more diverse guest list can promote more substantive and wide ranging discussions than are typically found on *Nightline* or *MacNeil/Lehrer*. Unfortunately, the *Kwitny Report*'s inability to attract renewed funding from corporate or foundation underwriters drove this valuable program off the air after its first and only season.

5

The Broken Promise of Public Television

(This chapter was written by David Croteau, William Hoynes, and Kevin M. Carragee)

From its beginning in 1967, the mission of public television has been to provide an alternative to commercial television and to reflect the diversity of the American public. The Carnegie Commission Report, which led Congress to pass the Public Broadcasting Act of 1967, argued that public television programming "can help us see America whole, in all its diversity," serve as "a forum for controversy and debate," and "provide a voice for groups in the community that may otherwise be unheard."[1] But in the more than 25 years since the Carnegie Report, numerous critics have suggested that public television provides a voice mainly for the left. Such attacks began as far back as the Nixon administration, when the president sought to veto all federal funding for public television in 1972.[2] That confrontation revealed how vulnerable public broadcasting was to political influence, because of its reliance on federal appropriations.

The Reagan administration also called for and obtained reductions in the funding of public television. One result was an increased reliance on corporate "underwriters" to fund public television. The percentage of public television's total budget that came from the federal government fell from 26 percent in 1980 to 16 percent in 1990, while corporate funding increased from 11 percent of the budget to 17 percent. By 1992, corporations had become the largest source of funds for programming produced by PBS's National Program Service, donating $90 million, or 30 percent of the whole—more than federal agencies and foundations combined.[3] It was in 1992 that the most visible attacks on public television took place.

This round of criticism was organized around two basic

themes. The first called for the elimination of public television altogether. Laurence Jarvik of the conservative Heritage Foundation was the most visible critic promoting this position. Jarvik's January 1992 report, "Making Public Television Public," was distributed by the Heritage Foundation and quoted widely in the news media.[4] In it Jarvik argued, contrary to the title of the report, for the *privatization* of public television. The rationale for such a move was twofold: (1) television, in principle, should be a private enterprise; and (2) public television has outlived its usefulness. The argument that television should be a private enterprise is based on the belief that audiences, through ratings, should determine the need for programs. The absence of such market forces leads to "elite" programming without a popular audience. The argument that public television has outlived its usefulness is based on the belief that new cable technologies have opened up television to the kinds of diverse quality programming that public television was meant to provide. Since such programming now exists on commercial television, the argument proceeds, there is no longer a need for public television.

This line of reasoning ignores the constraining impact of market forces on programming. *More* programming does not ensure *diverse* programming. It also ignores the high cost and limited availability of cable programming. As of 1992, only 60 percent of households even had *basic* cable service and only 28 percent had the more expensive "premium" cable channels.[5] Finally, Jarvik's position ignores the degree to which cable services have been dominated by entertainment, not public affairs, content.

The second theme sounded by conservative critics was limited to program content. David Horowitz of the Committee for Media Integrity (COMINT) argued that public television had a left-wing bias. In particular, Horowitz claimed that public television provided a forum for "the discredited pro-Soviet Left"[6] in its treatment of foreign policy issues, charges that were widely repeated as the debate ensued. On a similar note, Robert Knight of the Family Research Council argued that public television"is consistently antifamily, it favors alternative lifestyles and is usually a mirror of the liberal democratic agenda."[7] As a result, Horowitz and his allies argued that public television should be subject to more political control to ensure objectivity and balance. This claim of "bias" lies at the heart of all conservative critiques of public television—whether aimed at controlling programming or at eliminating the system altogether.

This position found powerful allies in Congress. Senate minority leader Robert Dole said on the Senate floor, "I have never been more turned off and more fed up with the increasing lack of balance and the unrelenting liberal cheerleading I see and hear on the public airwaves."[8] Dole charged that "the broadcasting apologists are hiding behind Big Bird, Mr. Rogers and *Masterpiece Theatre*, laying down their quality smokescreen while they shovel out funding for gay and lesbian shows."[9]

Much of the criticism focused on individual programs: United States Senator John McCain criticized the documentary *Maria's Story* for showing "the Communist guerillas in El Salvador in the most heroic of depictions." U.S. Senator Jesse Helms criticized the documentary *Tongues Untied*, which he said "blatantly promoted homosexuality as an acceptable lifestyle."[10]

While conservative efforts, led by Senators Helms and Dole, to cut or even eliminate federal funding for public broadcasting ultimately failed, the focus on the alleged lack of balance did have important consequences. The Public Telecommunications Act of 1992 directed the Corporation for Public Broadcasting to review public broadcasting programming annually to ensure "objectivity and balance in all programs or series of programs of a controversial nature."[11] The driving force behind this call for an annual review, and for the taking of "remedial" steps to correct any perceived imbalance, was the conservative claims of left-wing bias on public television.

Conservative critiques are misleading, however, in part because they have been based on a too narrow segment of public television programming. For example, the 1992 round of conservative critiques of public television often relied upon a study distributed by the Center for Media and Public Affairs, written by Robert and Linda Lichter and Daniel Amundson. This study, "Balance and Diversity in PBS Documentaries,"[12] suggested that despite difficulties in labelling a diverse set of topics and ideas as liberal or conservative, "…there can be little doubt that the ideas expressed on public affairs issues were far more consonant with the beliefs and preferences of contemporary American liberals than with those of conservatives."

But in fact, the study acknowledged that "many more hours of programming are offered to viewers by public broadcasting each year than any study could hope to analyze" and it went on to examine only a tiny slice of PBS programs. It did so by systematically excluding the bulk of programs broadcast by PBS stations. First, the study limited itself to "public affairs documentaries aired during the evening" over a one-year period between 1987 and 1988. This effectively eliminated the vast majority of public affairs programs broadcast on public television, including news, talk shows, and business programs. (The rationale for the exclusion of interview programs, talk shows, and panel discussions was that the *content* of such programs is not controlled by the producer. However, this ignores the basic fact that decisions concerning *who* to allow to speak on such programs is clearly in the hands of program producers.)

Second, the study broke down the documentaries examined into 35,094 small "segments" and then went on to ignore *98.3 percent* of these segments. It claimed that only 1.7 percent of the segments "clearly stated a thematic argument." Thus, this discussion of "balance" in PBS documentaries is, in fact, based on this tiny percentage of documentary programming—a genre of programming which, in turn, makes up only a small percentage of the overall schedule.

Finally, the Lichter, Lichter, and Amundson study explored PBS public affairs programming by sampling only one station, WETA in Washington, DC. This decision was made despite the authors' acknowledgment that "[t]here is no rigid, uniform PBS national broadcasting schedule;" it ignores the fact that the viewing opportunities and experiences of individuals in other PBS markets may be substantially different. Indeed, our analysis reveals considerable variability in the public affairs programming broadcast by different PBS stations. This variability has been ignored by the Lichter, Lichter, and Amundson study and by nearly all other critics of PBS.

Since critics often have been interested only in the "controversial" topics on public television, they have focused on a narrow selection of public affairs programs. As this study will show, this ignores the vast majority of what PBS stations air. This study also examines public affairs programming as a subsection of the public television schedule—but only after examining the scope of public television programming in general.

The Public TV Schedule

Relying on only a few programs to make broad assertions regarding public television, as conservative critics often have done, can only lead to distortion. It is important, then, to better describe the range of public television programming as experienced by viewers. The first part of this study analyzes the broader public television schedule.

Since local station managers determine what is aired on the 300-plus local stations that make up the PBS system, it is impossible to rely upon a single station's schedule to determine public television programming. We therefore chose 10 geographically varied metropolitan markets to include in our sample: Atlanta; Boston; Chicago; Denver; Houston; Kansas City; Los Angeles; Minneapolis; New York City; and Washington, D.C.

These markets include 24 percent of the entire U.S. viewing population, and feature five PBS "flagship" stations (Boston's WGBH, Chicago's WTTW, Los Angeles' KCET, New York's WNET and Washington's WETA), which produce much of the programming distributed throughout the system.

For our sample period, we randomly selected one week out of each of the first six months of 1992: Jan. 5-Jan. 11; Feb 9-Feb. 15; March 1-March 7; April 5-April 11; May 3-May 9; June 28-July 4. For these dates, we examined evening programming in an "expanded prime-time" period of 6:00 p.m. to midnight. This period includes the time of highest viewership—the evening audience for public television is twice the size of the daytime audience[13]—and, with the exception of children's programming, includes nearly all of public television's best known shows.

We then examined the television schedules in each market for these time periods, as printed in local newspapers, and categorized programs by type. Less than 1 percent of programs were unidentifiable, usually because programming was listed as "to be announced."

Five of the 10 markets we studied are served by two public television stations (for a total of 15 stations in the sample). When there were two stations in a market, we determined the program minutes of each station, then combined them to come up with a single "average" market schedule. We then averaged all the markets' results to construct a composite "national" public television schedule.

Analyzing the Schedule

Table 5.1 shows that more than half (59 percent) of public television's evening programming was given to national, *non*-public affairs programming. This category includes such diverse programming as dramas and comedies, music and dance programs, and non-public affairs documentaries such as travel programs.

National public affairs programs constituted 33 percent of the public television evening schedule, with news making up more than a third of this category (12 percent of the total). Current public affairs documentaries were 8 percent of programming, business and financial programs 5 percent, historical documentaries 4 percent and interview and talk shows 2 percent.[14]

Although the system is intended to reflect the local needs of communities, local programming comprised only 7 percent of evening airtime in the period we examined. This raises questions about public television's ability to examine local political debates and respond to the needs of diverse local communities.

The 10 nationally distributed programs that received the

Table 5.1

"National" PBS Programming:
Type of Program as Percentage of Air-Time*

Public Affairs	**33.2%**
News	12.1
Current Public Affairs Documentary	8.4
Business and Financial	4.6
Historical Documentary	4.4
Interview/Talk/Analyses	2.4
Other Public Affairs	1.3
Non-Public Affairs	**58.6%**
Drama and Comedy	18.4
Music and Dance	11.1
Non-Public Affairs Documentary	10.5
Nature	6.9
Scientific/Technical Documentary	5.7
Skills/Hobbies	3.1
Other Non-Public Affairs	3.0
Local	**7.3%**
Local Public Affairs	5.2
Local Non-Public Affairs	2.2
Local Unknown	0.0
Unknown	**0.8%**

*Figures may not add up to 100% due to rounding.

Table 5.2

Top Ten National Public Television
Programs by Air-Time

Program Name	Total Minutes of Air-Time*	% of Total Air-Time	# of Stations (of 15)
1) *MacNeil-Lehrer NewsHour*	24180	10.8	14
2) *Nightly Business Report*	7080	3.2	8
3) *NOVA*	5040	2.2	14
4) *Frontline*	4290	1.9	14
5) *Moyers' Listening to America*	2640	1.2	14
6) *Wall $treet Week*	2460	1.1	12
7) *American Experience*	2370	1.1	14
8) *Washington Week in Review*	2130	1.0	12
9) *Madness*	2010	0.9	13
10) *Machine that Changed the World*	1920	0.9	14
	54300	24.3%	

*This figure is total air time on all 15 stations in the sample

most airtime (on all 15 stations collectively) during our sample period are listed in Table 5.2. Collectively, these 10 programs constituted nearly a quarter (24 percent) of all evening airtime. The daily, hour-long *MacNeil/Lehrer NewsHour* tops the list with more than three times as much airtime as the second program, the daily, half-hour *Nightly Business Report.*

Conservative critiques of public television have usually been directed at only a few public affairs documentaries. However, all public affairs documentaries taken together make up only a small percentage (8 percent) of the evening schedule on PBS stations. Besides ignoring the majority of programming that is not about public affairs, these critiques also have tended to ignore the portion of public affairs programming that reflects established institutional interests, such as the business and finance programs.

Sources on Public Affairs Programs

Examining the scope of programming available on public television helps to put in perspective those critiques that are based on only a small part of the broadcast schedule. However, since public affairs programs have been the focus of so much debate, it is also necessary to examine those programs in detail.

It is virtually impossible to quantitatively measure the political "bias" of the news media in any meaningful way. The subjectivity inevitably involved in efforts to code stories, images, or statements on any left-right or liberal-conservative axis renders such efforts problematic. It often turns out that political "bias" is in the eye of the beholder. A more reliable method of assessing the politics of news programming is to examine the diversity of the sources. Once we determine whose voices are heard, and in what proportion, we can make inferences about the political content of public television.

Our examination of source patterns is for national public affairs programs, inclusively defined as all programs that appeared in two or more of the 10 markets in our study.

Our data set, however, was limited by the availability of printed transcripts. As a rule, those programs that were one-time specials were not available in transcript form. Transcripts were available, however, for almost all of the regular, national public affairs programs. (The one major exception was *Tony Brown's Journal*.)

Our analysis, then, focused on the 15 regular public affairs programs listed in Table 5.3, representing four different program types: news, business, talk/interview, and documentary. Any individual edition of a particular program had to be broadcast on at least two stations during our study period to be included in our sample. (For example, a repeat showing of *The American Experience* that aired in only one market would not be included.)

Table 5.3

Public Television Programs in Sample

Program Name	Program Type	# Eds.	Broadcast Freq.
MacNeil/Lehrer NewsHour	News	30	daily (weekdays)
Nightly Business Report	Business	30	daily (weekdays)
Adam Smith's Money World	Business	6	weekly
Firing Line	Talk/interview	6	weekly
Frontline	Documentary	6	weekly
McLaughlin Group	Talk/Interview	6	weekly
Wall $treet Week	Business	6	weekly
Washington Week in Review	Talk/Interview	6	weekly
Listening to America	Documentary	5	weekly (1992 only)
American Experience	Documentary	4	weekly
P.O.V.	Documentary	4	periodically
McLaughlin's One on One	Talk/interview	2	weekly
Health Quarterly	Documentary	1	quarterly
Moyers	Documentary	1	periodically
Learning in America	Documentary	1	periodically

Overall, we analyzed 114 separate programs, which included a total of 423 stories and 1,644 sources. All stories were coded by topic and geographic location; all on-camera sources, whether taped or live, were coded for sex, nationality, occupational status, political party, institutional affiliation and amount of participation, as measured in uniform transcript lines.[15] Program hosts and journalists who narrate their own reports were not included as sources.

Seventeen percent of the sources were "live" sources, appearing in discussion or interview segments on shows like

MacNeil/Lehrer, Nightly Business Report or *The McLaughlin Group.* The remaining 83 percent appeared on taped reports.

Despite the fact that "live" sources were only 17 percent of source appearances, they accounted for more than half of the airtime. These sources were allotted much more time to air their perspectives and had far more control over what viewers would hear them say than those sources who appeared in edited, taped reports.

Gender Imbalance

Male sources outweighed female sources in both frequency and volume of appearance by a ratio of 3 to 1. Men were nearly 77 percent of all sources, and 79 percent of sources who appeared "live."

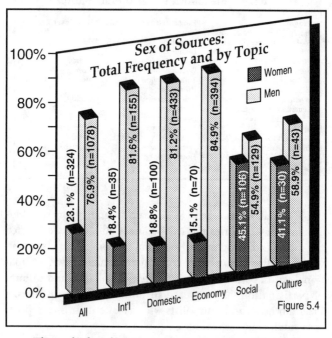

Figure 5.4

The male-female source ratio, however, varied across topics. As Figure 5.4 illustrates, female sources were more than twice as likely to appear in segments about social and cultural issues as in segments about international affairs, domestic politics and economics. As on network television, the inclusion of female voices is weighted more heavily toward "soft" news, leaving little room for the voices of women in discussions of the economic and political policy debates of the day.

The percentage of female sources also varies substantially across type of program, as Figure 5.5 shows. Women were much more likely to appear in documentary programs than other genres (36 percent of sources), and were particularly underrepresented in business programs (11 percent of sources, less than 6 percent of "live" sources).

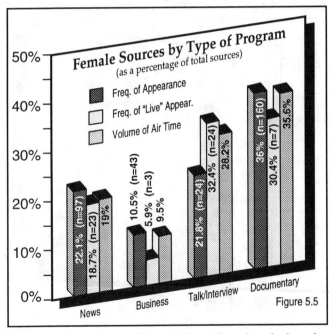

Figure 5.5

This variability can be partially attributed to the broader range of topics that the documentaries cover, including more social and cultural issues. It also may reflect the tendency of news and business programs to rely on sources connected to major political or economic institutions, who are disproportionately male. Still, the gender composition of public television sources is the result of choices made by producers and reporters, not some immutable law of broadcast journalism.

Public TV "Experts"

We also examined the occupational status of public television sources; the findings are summarized in Figure 5.6. Public television relied heavily on professional "experts": largely other journalists (12 percent of total sources) and academics (6 percent). Professionals accounted for less than one-third of source appearances, but took up almost half of the airtime and constituted almost three-fifths of the "live" appearances.

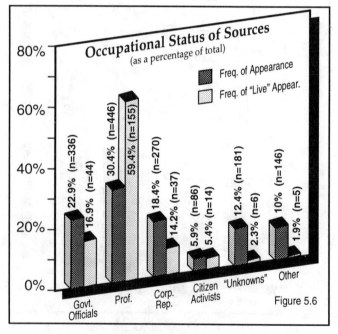

Figure 5.6

Government officials accounted for 23 percent of appearances. Professionals and government officials together took up more than 70 percent of airtime.

More than any other news outlet, public television is known for "expert" analysis of the political world. At its best, this approach allows for various interpretations of issues and events, not just the official interpretation.

However, public television's "experts" did not reflect diverse interests, but came largely from mainstream news organizations and thinktanks. The principal source of public television's "experts" were the mainstream daily newspapers and weekly newsmagazines, including the *New York Times*, *Wall Street Journal*, *Washington Post*, *Los Angeles Times*, *Chicago Tribune*, *Newsweek*, *Time* and *U.S. News & World Report*, along with the centrist journal of opinion, *The New Republic*.

MacNeil/Lehrer's regular feature, "Gergen and Shields," was the prototype here: The moderate conservative from *U.S. News & World Report* and the "liberal" from the *Washington Post* represented this narrow version of a "debate" between opposing sides. Other programs, including *Washington Week in Review* and *The McLaughlin Group*, provided similar "debates," usually between insiders that spanned the range from centrist to conservative.

Corporate Voices

There are two important differences between public television's sources and the findings of previous research on news sources. Both corporate representatives and members of the "general public" (sources such as voters, victims and "persons on the street") accounted for a larger percentage of sources than in previous analyses.

Our previous studies of ABC's *Nightline* and PBS's *MacNeil/Lehrer NewsHour* found that corporate representatives accounted for approximately 6 percent of the total sources. In all of public television's public affairs programs, corporate representatives appear three times as frequently (18 percent) and take up 12 percent of the airtime largely because of the business programs that are a regular part of the public television schedule.

The sheer frequency of corporate representatives is striking— they appeared half again as often as journalists, and three times as often as academics. The business shows provided these corporate voices with routine opportunities to interpret the political and economic scene.

The General Public

Members of the general public appeared in substantial numbers on public television. Their comments were used in a variety of settings, on a range of issues, providing an appearance of broad public involvement. However, as Figure 5.6 indicates, the level of "general public" participation suggested by the frequency of appearance is largely illusory.

While members of the "general public" made up over 12 percent of the sources, they accounted for less than 4 percent of air time, indicating that their appearances were usually brief, often reactive statements, rather than discussions or analyses. And members of the general public virtually never appear as "live" sources—the sources that have both more time and more control over how their views are presented.[16]

The brief statements of "public" sources in public television programming were typically used to personalize the issues or events that a news story or documentary was exploring. For example, a very short soundbite by an unemployed steel worker would serve to link the discussion of the competitive status of the U.S. steel industry to U.S. workers. Members of the public did not often appear as political actors; instead, their comments generally spoke to their immediate experience, and efforts to analyze this experience were left to professionals—journalists and academics.

Citizen Activists

On public television's public affairs programming (as in previously studied news outlets like *Nightline*, *MacNeil/Lehrer* and National Public Radio[17]), citizen activists make up about 6 percent of sources—a fraction of the number of government officials, professionals and corporate representatives. Even this figure may be misleading, for these activists represented a diverse set of interests, abortion opponents, labor representatives, environmentalists, supporters and opponents of David Duke, representatives of various racial and ethnic groups, and "good government" activists.

No one activist constituency accounts for more than a handful of sources. Labor representatives accounted for 0.9 percent of sources, racial/ethnic group representatives 1.6 percent, environmentalists 0.6 percent and feminists 0.2 percent. There were no representatives of gay or lesbian organizations in the sample. These findings stand in stark contrast to the conservative claim that public television provides a consistent platform for liberal or leftist activists. Actually, representatives of organizations that might challenge the boundaries of consensus politics appeared as sources so infrequently that many viewers might never see them.

The total absence of gay or lesbian activists during our sample period (out of 1,644 sources) highlights the problem with the conservatives' selective critique of public television. Conservative critics pointed to the program *Tongues Untied*, Marlon Riggs' exploration of the lives of gay black men, as evidence of the takeover of public television by "extremist groups." This focus on *Tongues Untied*, in fact, effectively obscured the larger source patterns on public television, in which representatives of gay and lesbian organizations were virtually invisible.

While there are exceptions—an edition of *Adam Smith's Money World* on the timber industry that featured environmentalists; an episode of *Listening to America* on government ethics that included both members of Congress and representatives of the public interest group Common Cause—public television did little to highlight the voices of organized citizens, relegating activists along with members of the general public to the margins of political discourse.

Sources in Different Forums

Professionals were the dominant source, as Table 5.7 shows, in both frequency of appearance and volume of air time, for coverage of all topics except for economic issues. In economic coverage, it was corporate representatives, not journalists and academics, who were the prime "experts." Corporate spokespersons constituted 44 percent of sources in economic stories, while activists accounted for 3 percent, and the "general public" 5 percent. (Non-professional workers accounted for 5 percent and small business people 1 percent of sources.)

Table 5.7

Source Occupational Status by Story Topic: Frequency of Appearance and Volume of Air Time
(column percentages)

	Intl.	Dom. Pol.	Econ.	Social	Culture
Govt Official (freq)	26.0%	31.3%	16.1%	17.1%	2.5%
(volume)	30.9%	29.1%	13.7%	22.2%	1.3%
Professional (freq)	40.0	36.5	23.2	36.7	65.8
(volume)	47.4	51.9	31.5	48.0	75.6
Corp. Rep. (freq)	10.5	4.4	44.4	1.9	3.8
(volume)	6.5	2.6	40.8	0.8	1.3
Citizen Activ. (freq)	2.5	8.7	3.1	7.6	0
(volume)	3.6	10.2	3.6	7.5	0
"Gen. Public" (freq)	6.5	11.9	5.0	23.3	26.6
(volume)	3.0	2.2	4.4	11.8	20.0
Other (freq)	14.5	7.2	8.2	13.4	1.3
(volume)	8.6	4.0	6.0	9.7	1.8

Members of the general public appeared most, in both frequency and volume of air time, in segments about social and cultural issues, generally in discussions that were not defined as policy-oriented.

The four types of programs also varied in the occupational profile of their sources as Table 5.8 shows. Government officials provided more than one-quarter of the sources on news and talk/interview programs, but accounted for only 17 percent of the sources on documentaries.

Professionals accounted for more than half of the guests on talk/interview programs. These shows are the domain of public television's political pundits—mostly journalists—who interpret current events. These pundits, however, represent a narrow spectrum of opinion. With the exception of *Washington Week in Review*, which relies upon prominent mainstream journalists, public television's political talk shows are hosted by well-known conservatives William F. Buckley (*Firing Line*) and John McLaughlin (*The McLaughlin Group, One on One*).

Corporate representatives constituted half of the sources on business programs, the same programs with the smallest representation of "unofficial" sources (citizen activists and the

Table 5.8

Occupational Status of Sources by Program Type
(column percentages)

	News	Business	Talk/Int	Documentary
Govt Official (freq)	27.8%	22.4%	28.0%	17.1%
(volume)	32.5%	14.9%	13.4%	18.7
Professional (freq)	30.9	19.7	54.2	34.1
(volume)	46.5	28.5	72.7	43.6
Corporate Rep (freq)	9.1	50.0	5.6	2.6
(volume)	5.4	52.3	5.3	2.2
Citizen Activ (freq)	5.8	2.4	3.7	9.6
(volume)	6.8	1.8	4.2	10.9
"Gen. Public" (freq)	14.2	2.6	5.6	20.8
(volume)	3.0	1.2	1.5	12.5
Other (freq)	12.2	2.9	2.9	15.8
(volume)	5.8	1.3	2.9	12.1

"general public"). Documentaries, on the other hand, had the smallest percentage of corporate representatives and were the site where citizen activists and the public had the most access.

Documentaries had the most variability in their sources: While professionals (again, largely journalists and academics) and government officials accounted for one-half of the sources, citizen activists and the "general public" were also regular sources. Perhaps the diverse sources—highlighting "unofficial" perspectives, with little reliance on corporate voices—is one of the reasons why documentaries have been the focus of political pressure from conservatives.

Republicans Versus Democrats

While we avoided subjective measurements of political slant, we did compare the relative frequency of Republican and Democratic politicians. Overall, use of Republican sources outweighed Democratic sources by 53 percent to 43 percent, a finding in sharp contrast to the conservative claim that public television public affairs programming is characterized by a "liberal bias." (The independent politicians appearing were nearly all affiliated with Ross Perot.) The Republican edge was at least partially the result of the heavy focus on then-President Bush, who was by far the single most frequently used source (39 times; candidate Bill Clinton was next with 16 appearances).

The slight Republican majority was consistent across almost all of the public affairs programs. In fact, of all those programs that regularly made use of politicians (five or more appearances), only *The McLaughlin Group* used Democrats more frequently than Republicans (59 percent/41 percent), nearly all of which were in the form of short soundbites from various Democratic Presidential primary candidates.

Even *Frontline* (53 percent/47 percent) and *Listening to America* (64 percent/36 percent), two programs that were the focus of political criticism by Republicans, made use of Republicans more frequently than Democrats. On documentaries, which have faced the toughest political pressure from conservatives in Congress, Republican sources outweighed Democratic sources in both frequency of appearance (59 percent/41 percent) and volume of airtime (63 percent/37 percent).

Missing Voices

To the extent that perspectives are underrepresented on public television, it is the same voices that are largely excluded from commercial news and public affairs programs: the voices of those who do not wield power or influence in society.

As we have noted, conservative complaints focus almost exclusively on documentary programs, and effectively exclude the vast majority of public affairs programming. Even so, there is little evidence that the documentaries themselves exhibit the kinds of political messages that recent critics have claimed. While unofficial sources, particularly those of citizen activists and members of the general public, have dramatically more access on documentaries, their perspectives (quite varied themselves) are paired with those of officials and traditional experts.

Why are documentaries held to different standards than other programs? Talk/interview programs are not generally singled out for the narrow spectrum of opinion they feature, or for the preponderance of conservative program hosts. Nor are business programs routinely criticized for their domination by corporate sources, who also happen to be the major financial backers of these programs. Our analysis suggests that the business program is, in fact, the most highly politicized type of program, overwhelmingly representing the interests of one social sector.

Race and the Game of Politics

Like *MacNeil/Lehrer*, public television talk and documentary programming usually took statements of government officials or politicians as the news peg of a story, and then analyzed the motives and efficacy of government action or political strategy. According to this reportorial frame, political actions frequently are motivated by strategic considerations and hidden agendas. The journalists and academics routinely employed as news sources on *MacNeil/Lehrer*, *Washington Week in Review* and *The McLaughlin Group* explored the opaque, indeed at times deceptive, nature of American politics.

The focus on "inside politics," however, has its costs. The continued emphasis on political strategy, calculation and tactics diverts attention from the substance of political actions and policies. Politics becomes a strategic game and news becomes a scorecard by which to asses the moves of its key players.

The Blame Game

Much of the coverage of the events in Los Angeles examined the debate concerning the assignment of responsibility for the riot and the political ramifications of the violence. Three programs—the *MacNeil/Lehrer NewsHour*, *The McLaughlin Group* and *Washington Week in Review*—explicitly define this as the "blame game." According to these programs, the blame game initially was linked to the charges by the Bush Administration that "failed" Great Society programs had contributed to urban decay and to the violence. For example, the *MacNeil/Lehrer NewsHour* reported on statements by Attorney General William Barr and Presidential Press Secretary Marlin Fitzwater linking the events in Los Angeles to allegedly misdirected social programs of the 1960's and 1970's:

> William Barr: I think what we're seeing in the inner
> city communities are essentially the grim harvest of
> the great society.
> Marlin Fitzwater: We believe that many of the root
> problems that have resulted in inner city difficulties
> were started in the '60's and '70's (5/8/92).

The degree to which the coverage focused on the blame game and these Republican charges documents the ability of the White House to shape both news coverage and public discourse. The Bush Administration was able to influence reporting on the aftermath of the Los Angeles violence by attacking Democratic policies of the past.

This framing of the Los Angeles events is contested by Democratic politicians. The programs afforded Democratic politicians, including Senators Bradley and Moynihan, an opportunity to rebut this interpretation. In turn, the Democrats proposed a counterframe: the violence in Los Angeles is a product, in part, of the years of neglect of urban and racial problems during the Bush and Reagan administrations. News analysis and interpretation, then, centers on these competing claims by government officials and on the likely political ramifications of this debate.

The definition of the blame game and the manner in which it influenced reporting and analysis is illustrated by the questions posed by John McLaughlin to his panel of journalists.

> McLaughlin: Issue one, the blame game....
> McLaughlin: How do you rate George Bush's handling of
> this crisis and of the blame?...
> McLaughlin: Let's talk more about George Bush's
> response to the riot and the political fallout....
> McLaughlin: .... is the political impact of Los Angeles as
> things stand now, a net plus or net minus for George

Bush? I ask you.... (5/8/92).

Similar, though admittedly less terse, framing of the blame game occurred on *Washington Week in Review* and the *MacNeil/Lehrer NewsHour*.

The considerable coverage devoted to the blame game highlights an ongoing focus of regular public television news programming: political strategy and tactics. Much of the analysis and reporting centers on who will win the blame game and how this likely will influence the presidential election of 1992. While assessments of the winners and losers of the game vary across programs and analysts, the emphasis on the strategic game of politics remains. Within this context, the events in Los Angeles derive much of their significance because of their political implications. The reportorial emphasis on the blame game, however, restricts coverage of the complex connections between the events in Los Angeles and issues related to race, class and the problems of American cities.

There is an added complexity to coverage of the blame game. Journalists and analysts examine the blame game, but have a distaste for it. This distaste becomes evident in a variety of forms. The very description of the political debate as the blame game delegitimizes it as a significant topic. Despite the relentless focus of John McLaughlin on the political implications of the blame game, Clarence Page, a participant in the program, stated "...this blame game is kind of silly and it's not only silly but it's destructive right now at a time when we should be pulling together" (5/8/92). A regular contributor to *Washington Week in Review*, Haynes Johnson, responded to a summary of Republican charge and Democratic countercharge concerning the policies of the 1960's and 1980's by saying "Who's talking about the '90's?" (5/8/92). After previously deploring the lack of attention to the substantive issues and problems highlighted by the violence in Los Angeles, Jim Lehrer returned to the blame game: "Everybody says, all right, the blame game is over. But the fact is the blame game, whether they play it or not, is never quite over in the minds of voters. At this stage of the game, who won it, do you think, or who's ahead?" (5/8/92).

There is a contradictory reportorial stance here: the blame game diverts attention away from the serious issues of race that need to be examined; but the game and its political implications will be examined in any case. Within this reportorial frame, the blame game is a deeply unfortunate continuation of "politics as usual" at a time of major significance. The attention devoted to the blame game, despite reservations about its significance, reveals the strong degree to which many regularly scheduled programs on PBS stations are committed to a focus on "inside politics."

Sources and Silences in Coverage of Los Angeles

The sourcing patterns employed in race-related coverage correspond to our broader findings concerning the degree to which varied actors have access to news as a social resource. A variety of political actors do speak, but these sources are primarily politicians, journalists and academics. The voices of inner city minority residents are seldom heard; most often their views are presented in very short sound bites which set the framework for an analysis of what these voices *really* mean.

As a consequence, reporting and analysis on the Los Angeles violence provides a narrative *for* and *by* professionals and government officials. The "story" of the black poor in cities, for example, is told by journalists and academics for an audience largely divorced from this experiential world. In this sense, the poor in American cities are defined as subjects to talk about, a problem to be managed. They seldom appear as social actors in their own right. The repeated focus on professional analysis of the poor and of black youth in inner cities suggests that these groups are unable to articulate their own views about the social conditions they confront. Paradoxically, the coverage itself often silences the very groups who are defined as powerless by the journalists, politicians, and academics who regularly dominate public television news programming.

This outcome is, in part, a product of the style or format adopted by the regularly scheduled public affairs programming on PBS stations. *The McLaughlin Group* and *Washington Week in Review* present *journalistic* views on the news of the week. the *MacNeil/Lehrer NewsHour*, although a more broadly based program than the talk and analysis shows, remains dominated by guests drawn from the two major political parties, the academy, and journalism. In addition, the in-studio interview dominates *MacNeil/Lehrer* as a reporting form. At its best, it can provide insight on a range of issues, but its routine focus is on policymakers (for example, the program provided a detailed and illuminating interview with four city mayors detailing the problems they confront). *MacNeil/Lehrer*'s somewhat limited use of stories derived from the location of news events necessarily restricts the access of some sources to this program.

Given these limitations within regularly scheduled public television programming, the documentary form provides the most extensive access to a variety of sources. Indeed, Bill Moyers' *Listening to America*, "In Search of a Common Destiny" provided the most diverse set of views concerning the causes and significance of the violence in Los Angeles. Combining brief sound bites derived from news stories with a "town meeting" that included a socially and demographically diverse set of participants, this documentary provides a wider forum for the articulation of diverse views than other programs concerning the events in Los Angeles.

We share Daniel Hallin's view that journalism at its very best combines an examination of the lived experience of people with an analysis of the political, economic, and social context that shapes that experience.[18] Much of public television's coverage of race-related issues fails to realize this admittedly high standard. This failure is a product of a variety of factors, including the repeated focus on the strategic game of politics and the relatively narrow range of sources employed in the programs. While there are a few exceptions, most public television public affairs programs during our sample and, in particular, the programs examining the violence in Los Angeles, failed to provide a sense of the lived experience of those who confront racism or those who confront the problems within American cities

Business As Usual:
Public TV Coverage of Economic Issues

In economic life, each individual plays a variety of roles. As *workers*, people are affected by issues such as workplace conditions, pay and employment outlook. As *consumers*, we are concerned with issues of product safety, quality, cost and legal rights. As *investors*, people are interested in the performance of stocks, bonds, commodities, mutual funds and other investment alternatives. Finally, as *citizens*, we want to know about economic developments, such as the Savings & Loan crisis, that have an impact on the nation's economic climate and influence government policy. Media coverage of economic affairs ideally should address this whole range of economic roles and activity.

Public television's coverage of economic issues, however, greatly skews the relative importance of each of these roles. The great majority of public television's coverage of economic affairs speaks to an audience of investors. In contrast, very little coverage is aimed at people as workers, consumers or citizens, leaving viewers with a distorted vision of the economic sphere.

The overemphasis on investment can be seen by merely examining the programs that PBS stations offer. Close to 5 percent of public television's programming in our study was devoted to business and financial investment programming—*Nightly Business Report, Wall $treet Week with Louis Rukeyser*, and *Adam Smith's Money World*. Comparable specialized economic programming intended for citizens, consumers or workers was non-existent.

A national program that looked at the economy and the workplace each week from the perspective of employees rather than investors would likely be the target of critics who would call it "biased," "anti-business" or "pro-union."[19] But the dominance of the business perspective is so complete on public (and commercial) television that entire programs devoted exclusively to the perspective of business and investors seem natural.

The Recession Numbers

Our look at economic coverage focused on public television's handling of the recession, the issue that dominated the 1992 election. The vast majority of recession coverage came from two regular programs, *MacNeil/Lehrer* and *Nightly Business Report.* Recession coverage was nearly always tied to economic reports and focused on the basic question, "Is the economy getting better or worse?" Much of this coverage also examined the political implications of economic conditions on the presidential campaign of 1992.

Economic coverage was usually organized around numbers. *Nightly Business Report,* for example, devoted regular segments to "the numbers"—daily stock updates. And much of public television's economic coverage was pegged to the release of economic reports. While economic data is an important element of economic coverage, a review of the coverage for our sample period raises questions about how such data was handled.

Economic statistics—with little or no explanation or analysis—sometimes made up an entire story. This was typical of the *Nightly Business Report,* which is clearly aimed at an audience of investors already well-versed in the meaning of economic data. A typical *Nightly Business Report* story would toss around statistics like the "National Association of Purchasing Management Index" without a glance backward to see if viewers are following.

Contradictory assessments of the meaning of economic statistics were a common feature of the coverage. As Robert MacNeil (*MacNeil/Lehrer,* 7/2/92) commented to two economists giving opposing forecasts, "It sounds like you're not talking about the same country, you two." The mixed economic signals of this period, coupled with the journalistic "balance" that is often struck between pessimistic and optimistic analyses, may have merely reinforced for the viewer the notion that no one really knows what is happening.

In fact, one *MacNeil/Lehrer* story on the economy (3/6/92) was simply called "The Guessing Game." In it, analyst David

Wyss of DRI/McGraw Hill, admitted that his forecasts are partly based on evidence he gathers by going to the local mall. "I
come to the Burlington Mall, especially like at Christmastime,
just to see how many people are shopping. Is there a recovery in
consumer spending, or are the stores empty?" Correspondent
Paul Solman ended this report by saying he would "leave the
final word to John Kenneth Galbraith, who said long ago that
there are only two kinds of economists, those who don't know
the economic future and those who don't know they don't
know." Despite such observations, *MacNeil/Lehrer* and other
public television programs continued to rely heavily on the forecasts of economists and investment analysts.

Reliance on such traditional sources for economic analysis meant that sometimes important numbers were nowhere to
be found in the coverage. For example, while the official monthly unemployment rate was regularly reported, programs almost
never mentioned the number of underemployed (involuntary
part-time employees) and the number of "discouraged" workers
(those who want employment but have given up looking).
Doing so would give a better picture of the relative health of the
economy and might shed some light, for example, on the gulf
between the severity of the latest recession according to the
widely reported numbers and as experienced by the public.
Employment numbers also obscure the issue of the quality of
jobs, an issue examined in detail in Bill Moyers' documentary
Minimum Wages.

Other economic figures can be deceptive. For example,
some critics argue that the Gross National Product, the most
important measure of economic activity, is misleading since it
ignores issues such as income distribution and environmental
impact. In addition, reliance on investment numbers can contribute to a decidedly short-term vision of the economy, examining economic trends in quarters, months, weeks, days or, in
the case of stocks, even hours.

Numbers of limited value were sometimes relied upon
much too heavily. The most common example of this was the
assumption that a rise in the stock market is positive economic

news for the nation as a whole. This is not necessarily the case. For example, a rise in corporate profitability may be the result of a rise in productivity, which in turn may be accompanied by big lay-offs. Such a development is not an unequivocally positive development. In moments of candor, economists will mention this fact, as when David Resler of Nomura Securities noted on *MacNeil/Lehrer* (3/3/92): "I think there's something to realize about the stock market. We've had a 25 percent increase since the middle of 1989 when this, the economy really started to slow down, so through the period of contraction or slowing economic activity, stock prices were doing rather well. And, unfortunately, I don't think they're as reliable an indicator of the future as they might have been in the past." Such lessons seemed to be forgotten in most of public television's coverage of the economy.

Whose Perspective?

The mistaken equation of economic health with investment fortunes was partly the result of a failure to recognize differing interests in the economy. For example, as noted, the profitability of companies cannot be equated with the health of the economy if such profitability is achieved at the expense of workers through lay-offs or reduced wages.

Such reasonable observations are lost, though, on analysts and commentators who are overwhelmingly viewing the economy from the limited perspective of investors or corporations. Since economists and corporate representatives dominated the analysis of economic data, and consumer or labor representatives were virtually non-existent in this type of coverage, the equation of corporate profits with general economic health could go unchallenged. For example, Ed Hymen of ISI Group, a source on *Adam Smith* (2/6/92), was able to comment, uncontested: "Average hourly earnings is a gauge of how much people are getting in pay increase in their paycheck. It's up 3 percent. It's the smallest increase since the 1950's. It's great for inflation. If you're on the receiving end of it, you sure don't like it, but it is great for inflation. And in a global sense…it's the brightest spot the U.S. has because it makes the U.S. gain competitiveness."

While low wages may be a "bright spot" for investors, the economic world looks different from the perspective of workers. In *Minimum Wages*, Ellen Bravo of the labor organization 9 to 5 commented: "There was a conscious decision on the part of many business leaders—back in the mid-'70s, when the United States first started facing a lot of competition—to cheapen the workforce, that the way they would stay competitive was by lowering costs. And really, a lot of that meant labor costs. It meant investing overseas if they could get it. It meant making jobs part-time and temporary, getting rid of benefits, lowering wages, keeping the minimum wage low."

Such views from the perspective of labor representatives were largely absent in the regular *MacNeil/Lehrer* and *Nightly Business Report* coverage of the recession. Instead, the exclusively business and investment perspective on such programs could lead to unchallenged economic interpretations of Orwellian proportions. Such was the case with this analysis from James Grant, editor of *Grant's Interest Rate Observer*, on *Adam Smith* (2/6/92): "We've been living in a hall of mirrors where bad is good, a weak economy means low rates, low rates means high stocks and everyone is rooting for the very worst they can imagine. So, paradoxically, good might be bad so far as business is concerned."

Economic Programming and Sources

Given the limited range of economic programming regularly offered, it is no surprise that the sources used on economic stories are overwhelmingly corporate representatives (44 percent) and economists, usually from investment firms. Labor, consumer or public interest representatives were almost never featured on the regular economic programming. When they do appear on economic stories (3 percent of sources), they are more likely to be relegated to documentaries which appear irregularly.

Neither were ordinary citizens a prominent part of economic coverage, making up 5 percent of the sources. Comments from working people were nearly always limited to very short quotes, which were later analyzed and contextualized by experts. The Moyers special, *Minimum Wages*, was the dramatic exception in our sample, presenting diverse views on job quality from workers and labor representatives extensively, along with corporate spokespersons.

The difference between regular daily or weekly programs and the irregular documentaries is an important one. Corporate and investment voices receive extensive and regular access through the daily news and business programs. On the rare occasion when they did appear, workers, consumers and citizens' representatives were largely confined to irregular documentary programs, the very programs often attacked by conservatives.

Conclusion

Our findings cast considerable doubt on conservative claims concerning the liberal or left-wing bias of public television programming. For example, as our examination of sourcing patterns reveals, environmentalists, feminists and labor activists received scant attention within public television programming, while corporate and government spokespersons dominate regularly scheduled news and information programs.

Despite repeated claims by conservatives that public television programming provides a sympathetic definition of gay and lesbian life, our findings indicate that no gay or lesbian spokespersons received access to public television public affairs programming during our sample period.

The primary target of the conservative critique, public affairs documentaries, account for a small percentage of the overall public affairs lineup on PBS stations, a point that the conservative critics conveniently ignore. Finally, we found no evidence of a consistent liberal or left-wing bias in these documentaries.

The shortcomings of public television, our findings suggest, have little to do with the charges advanced by its vocal conservative critics. The challenges ahead for public television are to enhance the diversity of its programming and to refocus on the "public" that public television is intended to serve. On both counts, we find that there is significant room for improvement.

Since its inception, as the Carnegie Commission Report indicated, one of public television's principal goals has been to provide programs that are diverse in both content and authorship. Certainly, public television maintains this rhetorical commitment today. However, only one of the four genres of public affairs programming that PBS stations regularly carry exhibits any meaningful diversity, either demographically or politically: the documentary.

We should not overstate the case; while documentaries are far more diverse than the other public affairs programming, as a whole they still rely to a large extent on traditional news sources. Other public affairs programs—news, business and talk shows—are substantially lacking in diversity. They provide space for the traditional "newsmakers" and "experts" to interpret the world, much as commercial news media do.

Furthermore, it is not at all clear that public television provides programming for an engaged citizenry any more than commercial television does. One sign of this is the small amount of local programming that is broadcast—a genre that deserve closer attention than we were able to offer here. While this may be primarily the result of financial constraints, it is nevertheless surprising for a system that has long proclaimed its commitment to local communities.

Equally important is the fact that national public affairs programming presents politics as a strategic game to be interpreted by professional experts. When members of the public are afforded access to public television, their brief statements are generally subject to interpretation by the anointed experts, suggesting that ordinary Americans are subjects to be talked about rather than political actors in their own right.

Moreover, organized groups of citizens, regardless of their political stripe, are largely absent from public affairs programming. People without connections to establishment institutions are rarely seen as able to either articulate their views or organize themselves into a meaningful political force.

This definition of politics and of political action ill serves both the viewing public and democratic ideals. While this study refutes the conservative critiques of public television, it does point to more fundamental challenges confronting public broadcasting. Ultimately, providing room for a more diverse set of voices and giving the public broader access to the airwaves can only make public television a more vital and widely supported institution.

6
Response and Action

In a society where the media—especially television—are so pervasive, it would be foolhardy to ignore the potential impact of media on democratic politics. Citizens interested in any type of public policy or political issue will inevitably have to contend with the impact of the mainstream news media. Sometimes this influence is direct, as with coverage of a particular organization's activities. More often, the media's impact is diffuse, as with its broader shaping of public discourse about particular issues. Either way, citizen activists are usually aware of the potential repercussion of the mainstream media on their work.

Sometimes the primary response of activists to mainstream media is one of frustration. Too often the media seem to neglect significant issues, ignore important voices and perspectives, and take for granted assumptions which ought to be part of the public debate. Watching or reading mainstream media, then, can be quite vexing. It's no surprise, therefore, that many progressive activists rely on alternative media to learn more about their world and to reach a relatively narrow but sympathetic audience.

This final chapter is written with a special eye towards those who are interested in engaging the media, either on a particular issue of concern, or on more general grounds. Our intent is not to provide a "how to" guide, but rather to raise some broader questions of how active citizens might think of their relationship to both mainstream and alternative media. We begin this discussion by examining some of the media response to our work over the years. When the reports collected in this volume were initially released, they generated considerable media coverage and comment from journalists. This material provides a window into some of the dynamics involved in working with the media.

Responses to the Original Studies

The responses to our original studies can be loosely grouped under three headings. First, our methodological approach to studying media was criticized. Second, some commentary highlighted conflicting conceptions of "news." A third area of concern was how certain journalistic practices have contributed to the situation described in our reports. We will take up each of these topics below.

Before moving on to these issues, however, it is important to note the obvious: there *was* coverage of and response to these studies. Too often hard work by activists and researchers goes unnoticed by the media. In this case, though, many media outlets covered the release of the reports making the study's findings widely accessible. In so doing, a critique of the news media that challenges the conventional wisdom was at least briefly available to a public that is regularly bombarded by lamentations about the so-called liberal media. Such coverage, along with distribution of the findings in *Extra!*, provided potential resources for citizens with incipient criticisms of the media. There are a number of factors that contributed to this situation. Some of these had to do with our topic. The programs being discussed were well-known, some with celebrities at their helm. Our criticism was leveled at *television* news perhaps making it easier for print reporters to safely write about these studies. (There was almost no television coverage.) Some factors were logistical. As academics we worked with total freedom in doing the research and writing the reports, but we turned to the media watchdog group, FAIR, to release and distribute the studies. Their skill and energy in this area meant that work which otherwise might go unnoticed received considerable media attention.

Some columnists commenting on the studies were also supportive. Howard Rosenberg of the *Los Angeles Times* wrote of the *Nightline* study, "...the study is microcosmic, defining by implication a much larger arena of TV in which public affairs programs are too often cozy clubs where gentlemen gather to talk politics over brandy and billiards."[1] Some in the media also had a sense of humor. One story on our *Nightline* study was accompanied by an Associated Press photo of Ted Koppel with Kermit the Frog. The caption read, "Ted Koppel faces the camera during a rare appearance with a minority group member."[2]

The studies generated some response from those under scrutiny as well. For reasons we will discuss below, *Nightline* host Ted Koppel was critical of the report. But he also noted, "I like studies like this…. I'm happy to see them, whether they are from the right or the left. They do give us an opportunity to reexamine what we do, how we do it. And sometimes it's quite true we get into a rut."[3] *Nightline*'s executive producer, Richard Kaplan, told reporters that the study had generated much discussion among the program's staffmembers. He conceded that some of our criticisms were on the mark, noting "I think we have reported terrorism too narrowly, and we need to broaden our coverage" and "We need to bring opposing domestic viewpoints."[4] When his program came under scrutiny in our second study, *MacNeil/Lehrer*'s executive producer, Lester Crystal also criticized our work but acknowledged, "Range and diversity are very good objectives. We can and should do better."[5]

Despite such comments, there were no substantial changes in these programs. However, as we noted in Chapter 4, there seemed to be some *minimal* shifts in the pattern of *Nightline*'s guests. Shortly after the *Nightline* study was released, a representative from the Committee in Solidarity with the People of El Salvador (CISPES) was included in a discussion of elections in El Salvador, the first time that *Nightline* had provided access to CISPES.[6] Not long after our report on *MacNeil/Lehrer* was released, Erwin Knoll of the *Progressive* magazine became an occasional commentator on the program's regular discussion segment among journalists from around the country. Of course, in the larger scheme of public affairs television, these are trivial changes that leave intact all of the problematic practices we have discussed.

However, most of the response from those associated with the programs we studied was—understandably—critical. It is to these criticisms that we now turn.

Methodological Criticisms

There is an odd dilemma that faces individuals or groups who wish to engage in constructive media criticism. Most critiques of media coverage coming from activists or community members are easily dismissed as vague and impressionistic. Journalists expect a certain amount of criticism and reporters are unlikely to pay serious attention to claims that are not backed up by analysis and research. Part of our contribution to the media debate, we hoped, was to provide some solid data which could document media practices.

The fact that our reports were covered in the mainstream media speaks, in part, to the usefulness of having solid empirical evidence for our arguments. But the very concrete nature of our data was also used by *Nightline* executive producer Richard Kaplan to critique the study. Ignoring the qualitative case studies in our study, Kaplan told reporters, "…my basic objection is that they take *Nightline* and reduce it to a bunch of numbers."[7] In a similar vein, Robert MacNeil criticized our study of his program, arguing that we "went wrong in a number of ways. One is, like a lot of sociologists, they think that everything can be quantified and that you can analyze by quantity … and not qualitative analysis."[8] Meanwhile in writing about the PBS study, Karen Bedford, from *Current*, "The Public Telecommunication Newspaper," referred to the qualitative case studies as "the most subjective part of the study" and the head of PBS programming, Jennifer Lawson, called it "the weakest part of the report."[9]

Thus a basic dilemma is revealed. Critiques that do not have systematic analyses and research can be dismissed as simply impressionistic or a case of misperception. Even qualitative analyses face the charge of being "subjective." However, critiques that use content analysis techniques to develop solid quantitative evidence can be dismissed as just "a bunch of numbers." Damned if you do. Damned if you don't.

There is no simple way to overcome this dilemma. We are not naive about the likelihood that the evidence will "speak for itself." Because of their financial and political resources, conservative media critics—often with little or no evidence—have had a substantial impact on the debate about media politics. However, for progressives who lack insider political connections and substantial resources, convincing data may be the only way to get the attention of the media and, more importantly, the general public. If the goal is to have the media report on this evidence so that a critical analysis of news media reaches a larger public, it must fit into the brief story format that most journalists use. Inevitably, that means quantitative data is most likely to be used in media reports. While perhaps useful in summarizing findings for brief media stories, quantitative data can oversimplify the complex realities of media coverage. A more nuanced understanding is likely to result from qualitative analyses. That is why our reports have included both components. However, media accounts of our work have almost always highlighted quantitative data, while neglecting the more subtle arguments we were trying to make.

Taped Reports

Another methodological criticism of our first two studies was that we failed to consider taped segments shown on *Nightline* and *MacNeil/Lehrer*, focusing instead on the in-studio guests. Our rationale was that what made these programs unique was their regular use of such guests and that these guests—unlike those featured in taped segments—had more control over how their views were communicated since they were not subject to editing by producers. These "live" guests had much more airtime to explain their views. They could frame or re-frame questions and respond as they saw fit. Those contributing soundbites to taped segments were at the mercy of those who edited the piece. We remain convinced that the role of guests on programs like *Nightline* and *MacNeil/Lehrer* is their central defining characteristic.

Nightline personnel were correct that there is a slightly wider variety of perspectives on the taped background reports than in the program's guest list. Yet this only underlines our suggestion that more diversity is needed among the guests that populate the 12- to 15-minute discussion segment, the core of the show. It proves the *Nightline* staff knows there is a wider diversity of perspectives in the United States than is apparent in their guest list. Why, we wonder, should the views of critics of those in power be limited to ten-second sound bites on a background segment? Doesn't this imply that these views are less worthy of the public's attention?

We were also criticized for looking at *who* spoke on programs, rather than *what* they said. Ted Koppel, for example, argued that you can't conclude "that simply by looking at a guest list, you know what the substance of that program was."[10] However, we *did* look at what people said. The entire point of having case studies in each report was to move beyond only examining guest lists and to examine how key issues were framed on these programs. Of course, it is just such qualitative analysis which can be labelled "subjective."

This charge of subjectivity is one reason why our analysis of guest lists is so important. To our knowledge, no one has ever contested our findings about who was being invited to speak on the programs we studied. We were able, therefore, to provide some systematic, reliable evidence on a subject about which people often already had emergent ideas. If they were concerned about such issues, regular viewers may have had the *impression* that guests on TV public affairs programs had very restricted boundaries—but they had no way of identifying the way these limits were constructed. They may have had the *impression* that PBS featured many of the same types of people on its programming as the commercial network, but absent systematic analysis of the programming, there was no way of being certain of this.

Taken by itself, our work on guest lists was a limited analysis. That was why we supplemented this data with more nuanced case studies. However, the guest-list analyses were important in providing a foundation for discussion and debate. But data can only go so far. Our quantitative data may have been irrefutable, but the *meaning* of those findings was another area where there was considerable response to our work. These responses go to the heart of defining the concept of "news."

Debating the Concept of "News"

The limited range of guests featured on most television public affairs programs does not necessarily concern journalists and observers. It was clearly a major concern of ours and we tried to lay out why we thought it was important for the media in a democratic society to reflect the diversity in that society. Others disagreed.

Nightline host, Ted Koppel, for example, argued against the very premise of our criticism. He suggested, "Ours is a news program. It is not meant to be a forum to give all divergent views in the United States equal access."[11] Others argued similarly that such programs were not meant to be "op-ed" pages but rather the broadcast equivalent of the front page. But clearly both *Nightline* and the interview portions of *MacNeil/Lehrer* are *not* traditional news broadcasts. In fact, their niche in the market is that they allow for in-depth analysis and commentary, unlike regular news broadcasts. As we argued in the original studies, then, *who* is invited to provide such analysis and commentary becomes an especially important issue.

Even if one were to accept the dubious claim that these programs were offering "news" rather than analyses and commentary, such a perspective still begs the question: what is news? The answer, according to many in the media, is clear—and to our minds equally disturbing. For many in the mainstream media, "news" is about what those in power say and do.

News as the Actions of Powerful "Players"

One of the most interesting aspects of the response to our work was how it made explicit the usually hidden assumptions behind much news coverage. What came through loud and clear was that many journalists believe that, by definition, news is about the actions of those who wield power. Therefore, they were not surprised, nor were they disturbed, by our findings that the overwhelming majority of people featured on public affairs programs occupy positions of power and authority.

For example, *Nightline* executive producer Richard Kaplan argued, "We're a news show, not a public-affairs show. Our job is to bring on guests who make the news—the players, in other words. And with a conservative administration in Washington, most of those players happen to be white males."[12]

Ted Koppel made similar arguments, "When we are covering the news, we try to go to the people involved in the news. What they have reflected in their analysis of our guest list is that over the 40 months, we've been dealing with a rather conservative Reagan Administration. If we had a liberal administration in office you would suddenly see an enormous disparity in the other direction."[13]

This response sidesteps the substance of our critique of *Nightline*. The majority of the most frequent guests in that 40 month period—such as Kissinger, Haig, Falwell, and Lawrence Eagleburger—were *not* current government officials or decision-makers. What we discovered, instead, was a litany of "experts"—usually ex-officials-who largely supported the conservative government. (If former government service is a qualification for becoming a *Nightline* guest, the show could turn on occasion to dissident experts—such as ex-Attorney General Ramsey Clark, former military strategist Daniel Ellsberg, ex-CIA official John Stockwell, or former White House aide Midge Costanza.)

Still, others agreed with Kaplan and Koppel's line of reasoning. *New York Times* writer, Walter Goodman, wrote "These programs are not meant to be debating societies or incitements to emotion on the order of 'Oprah' and 'Donahue'; they are focused on policy decisions. As more women and minorities make their way into the halls of power, they will doubtless find themselves in television studios, too."[14]

Sometimes this sort of argument reached near-comic proportions. Laura Fraser wrote in the *San Francisco Bay Guardian*:

> Laura Wessner, *Nightline*'s press representative, told me that while 'the whole staff looked at the study and thought it was very important,' *Nightline* 'can't help it if the world leaders are white men.'
>
> She challenged me to come up with the names of

women who are powerful and important enough to put on *Nightline.* When I gave her several names off the top of my head—Eleanor Smeal, Faye Wattleton, Randall Forsberg, Barbara Ehrenreich, Frances Moore Lappe, Pat Schroeder—she mumbled something about how 'we haven't done shows on those topics.'

No kidding.[15]

The problem with this sort of analysis lies in the defining of news as being only about what those in power say and do. Fraser identifies the problem well, writing, "...this is a strange new definition of newsgathering. Up until now, I've always understood that newsgathering involves rounding up a few conflicting sources to try to piece together a reasonable version of the truth, not acting as a PR tool for one side, thereby enhancing the power of that (right-wing) side."[16]

As we have tried to argue, our vision of what constitutes quality media coverage is different from that in many newsrooms. We contend that the media need to pay attention to the perspectives and needs of those who are outside the halls of power along with those who currently appear in the media. Relying on government, corporate, and professional elites to define issues and provide commentary excludes the majority of the population and can only produce a limited picture of the social and political world.

Of course news must report on the significant actions of those in power. No one would contest this point. But what distinguishes a free press from one that is merely a mouthpiece for those in power is that it creates room for dissenting voices—for those who don't walk the halls of power, for those affected by decisions made in those centers of power, and for those who disagree with the assumptions of those in power. This is at the heart of our critique.

Journalistic Practices and the Limitation of Debate

As we have seen, many in the media believe news should be about the actions of those in power. They see no need to include voices of dissent or disagreement that emanate from outside of the circle of power. Dissenting voices are not necessary, it is argued, because journalists themselves can serve as devil's advocates asking "tough questions" of those in power.

This was a prominent feature of Ted Koppel's response to our work. He argued, "Never is it suggested that I might ask (the guests) a tough question once in a while. Never it is even suggested that if you want to critique U.S. foreign policy, you don't bring on the opponents of U.S. foreign policy and let them speak their minds. What you do is bring on the architects of U.S., foreign policy and hold them to account, which is what we try to do on this broadcast."[17] *Nightline* executive producer, Richard Kaplan, agreed, saying that government foreign policy makers were invited because they determine policy and "they're the ones whose feet we want to hold to the fire."[18]

It should be clear by now that we find this view fundamentally problematic. We contend that it is essential for diverse voices to be heard on television public affairs programs. It is not enough for journalists to paternalistically believe that they can serve as surrogates for dissenting voices in political debates. Such an approach suggests that, rather than investigating the different perspectives on a topic, journalists think they already understand the issues being examined. But those with differing views should be allowed to speak for themselves.

One newspaper editorial made the point well, noting "Gifted and well-briefed though he may be, an all-purpose celebrity host like Ted Koppel can't present the views of relevant uninvited specialists as well as they could themselves if they were actual guests, all made up and right on the show." The editorial went on to note that, "Many 'newsmakers' simply won't appear on television with an articulate adversary. The Reagan White House had a full-time TV manager screen guests and questions in advance of administration officials' appearances on such programs as Mr. Koppel's."[19]

Koppel is certainly a more active interviewer than either Robert MacNeil or Jim Lehrer, and he asks more substantive questions. While he should be commended for this, it in no way renders critical experts unnecessary. In fact, Koppel's questions rarely reflect the concerns of opposition critics. During the years in which popular, independent movements challenged U.S. foreign policies regarding nuclear weapons and Central America, Koppel consistently failed to ask the questions posed by these movements. Instead, Koppel's "toughest" foreign policy questions often challenged hard-line White House spokespersons as to whether they were sufficiently hard-line.

The basic issues are simple: Who, except for an environmentalist, will raise pointed questions about corporate culpability for environmental decay? Who, other than a peace activist will raise fundamental questions about the history of U.S. government intervention in the Third World? More generally, who is going to raise questions about the underlying assumptions which *Nightline* and other media share? Even if tough questions are sometimes asked by Koppel, they are more likely to be shrewdly and vigorously pursued by a guest with an alternative perspective. The inclusion of critical voices is the surest way of guaranteeing a robust debate. The public has a right to hear these voices for themselves.

The inadequacy of relying on journalists to ask supposedly "tough questions" is coupled with what columnist Clarence Page called a "peculiar malady" of the media which he labelled the "Rolodex Syndrome." He observed, "For all the competition among the nation's news shops, there is precious little competition for new faces or viewpoints to illuminate old problems. In a pinch, editors and news directors are most comfortable with familiar names and faces. So, it is reasoned, are audiences."[20] A similar point was made by *Los Angeles Times* writer, Howard Rosenberg, suggesting that narrow guest lists are "less a matter of politics than of energy and enterprise, for the news media are basically lazy, often relying on quotable and dependable old standbys instead of taking the time to seek out new voices that could widen the debate."[21]

Finally, there was another interesting response to our studies which relates to journalistic practice. Some journalists used our criticism as evidence that the media are, in fact, doing a good, objective job. The logic goes something like this: if journalists are being criticized by conservatives for being too liberal and from liberals for being conservative, then they are being even-handed. For example, in responding to our study PBS spokeswoman Karen Doyne said, "We take it from both ends of the spectrum and the truth is exactly in between."[22]

This type of argument arose in relation to our work because of the involvement of the progressive media-watchdog group, FAIR. Some journalists tried to pair FAIR with Accuracy in Media (AIM), the conservative media watchdog organization. They implied that critiques distributed by FAIR were somehow balanced by those promoted by AIM, thus showing the media's balanced approach. *New York Times* reporter Walter Goodman wrote, "Now, if truth in advertising were in effect, Fairness and Accuracy in Reporting would have to acknowledge that it is not more interested in fairness than its right-wing counterpart, Accuracy in Media, is interested in accuracy. Both are players in the public-opinion game, advancing views that originate on the farther edges of America's political spectrum."[23] The implication, here too, was that the truth—and the media—are squarely in the middle.

Such an argument ignores the substantive differences in the agendas pursued by FAIR and AIM. They are not mere bookends on the political spectrum mirroring each other. At the very least, FAIR's calls are for more diversity and inclusiveness, while AIM's goals border on the censorship of ideas they find unacceptable. Journalists using this line of defense attempt to avoid addressing the content of critiques, staking their claim instead to a safe, mainstream middle ground.

Lessons and their Uses

The studies presented in this volume and the media responses they generated provide some lessons regarding the obstacles and opportunities facing citizens who work for a responsive free press. The most obvious lessons concern the obstacles that prevent more access to mainstream media for voices that do not represent powerful interests.

Journalistic practices as they are generally constructed

favor mainstream voices of power. When news is defined as what "players" do, most American citizens are left out. When "debate" is conceived of only as policy differences between Democrats and Republicans, many fundamental issues facing American society are ignored. Not the least of these issues is the growing frustration in many sectors of American society with those who wield power—whether Democrat or Republican— by those who do not. The growing alienation and cynicism of the American electorate towards politicians should be a clear indication that those in Congress do not adequately represent the views of many Americans. In the 1992 presidential election, Republican and Democratic voters *combined* made up a minority of the eligible American electorate. Most Americans didn't vote at all or they voted for "change" in the persona of Ross Perot. While there are many reasons for not voting, one of the most important is likely to be a perception that election results matter little when both the major party candidates represent similar interests.[24]

The media's structure as a for-profit industry also means that its concerns are not primarily with providing a public service, but rather with producing low-cost news that attracts an audience. Nowhere is this more apparent than in the competition between TV "news magazines" going on at this writing. These programs are cheap to produce and easily adaptable to stories of violence, crime, scandals, celebrities, and sex that draw high ratings. Given the success of these entertainment programs in the guise of "news," we are likely to see such ratings-driven programming become even more important in "regular" news programs.

The news media's status as part of corporate conglomerates means that while their reporting may occasionally embarrass some public officials and corporate representatives, they ultimately have a great deal in common with such interests. Their dependence on government officials as sources and potential regulators suggests, at the very least, that deference to such powers is prudent. The media's ownership by corporations with interests in far-ranging areas of politics and the economy, and their dependence on advertising by other corporations, means that pursuing corporate misdeeds might be counterproductive. It is difficult to imagine, for example, that the recent spate of unflattering television stories on the tobacco industry would have surfaced had the industry still been a major advertiser on network television.

Mainstream media outlets, therefore, are not likely to be regularly featuring the views of those outside a narrow consensus any time soon. But our work does help show where the most diverse sorts of programming—and the most opportunity—currently exists. Public television documentaries, for example, sometimes prove to be the exception to the rule. They offer brief glimpses of the world beyond the Washington-Wall Street corridor of power. They sometimes feature voices that are otherwise almost never heard on television. And for doing so, such programs draw the wrath of those who guard the status quo. Even here, however, the openings are small and temporary; they sometimes allow for more diverse content, but rarely provide access to a more diverse set of authors. Independent producers fighting for access to public television have traditionally had a difficult time getting through these closed doors. Much of television—including public television's news and public affairs programs—is a bland wasteland populated by politicians, professional "experts", and corporate spokespersons. But the unusual diversity sometimes found on public television documentary programs means that sweeping generalizations about mainstream media often hide more complex realities.

New media arenas—which were not part of our studies—also hold some potential for more diversity. Public access programs, some cable programming, and even some computer-based communications networks may come to play a significant role in the future in delivering more diverse debates and discussions. For now, though, they are still more potential than reality. Unfortunately, we suspect the economic forces that are likely to shape these new media will push them in a direction that will prove to be quite disappointing.[25]

Considering Media Politics:
Mainstream or Alternative?

We believe that the mainstream media are important in a democratic society. From the perspective of those organizing for social change, the media play several important roles.

First, the media serve the role of "agenda setter" by their coverage of political activities and issues. The mainstream media may not be able to tell people what to think, but it is likely to have a significant impact on what people think about. This is especially true when considering issues that are not in the immediate experience of people's daily lives.

Second, when the media do cover social and political issues, they must "frame" the discussion by highlighting certain aspects of a story and downplaying others, by providing or not providing certain background information, and so on. Activists attempting to mobilize parts of the general public need to be aware of how the issues they are working on have been portrayed in the mainstream media. They also need to be aware of what kinds of information people are likely to have, or not have, as a result of mainstream media coverage of the issue.

Finally, in framing an issue, the media have the power to legitimate or marginalize particular viewpoints and actors related to a story. Who is to be consulted for analysis and commentary on a subject? Whose views can safely be left out? Such decisions do not reflect an objective reality external to the journalistic process. Instead, they help to construct what is thought of as political and social reality.

Many activists are also concerned about the media because they believe that coverage can positively affect their political work. But, specifically, how can coverage by mainstream media ideally help movement efforts?

First, media coverage can expand the scope of the conflict. By expanding the scope of conflict and introducing new actors and resources, the "underdog" in a political contest can attempt to even the scales, so to speak. The media become important in this process. By receiving media coverage, social movements make others aware of their organizing efforts and of the issues

185

under contention. The aim from the point of view of these movements is to encourage new actors to enter the "fight" as allies. Conversely, powerful authorities have an interest in limiting the scope of conflict because they are better able to dictate the outcome as long as the conflict remains private.

Second, media coverage can help movements to attract resources and supporters, especially elites. For example, in the civil rights struggle against state and local injustices, the primary elite being courted by activists was the federal government. In Martin Luther King, Jr's words, "The key to everything is federal commitment." The civil rights movement was quite successful in soliciting the attention and help of the federal government. Very often this attention was catalyzed by dramatic media coverage.

The importance of media coverage in propelling a movement can also be seen in the fact that many successful tactics used by the civil rights movement were used unsuccessfully in earlier efforts which did not receive significant media attention. Thus the now-famous 1960 Greensboro lunch-counter sit-ins were preceded in 1957 and 1958 by very similar efforts in Oklahoma and Kansas. The 1955-56 Montgomery bus boycott was modeled after a lesser known, although somewhat successful, 1953 boycott in Baton Rouge. While other factors certainly came into play, the inability of these earlier efforts to generate widespread media coverage contributed to their limited impact.

Third, in addition to directly generating legislative, financial, and other support from elites, media coverage of a social movement can also aid in education and recruitment efforts. However, the benefits of membership recruitment through mass media should not be exaggerated. As an anonymous author in one civil disobedience handbook puts it, "It is clear that the media can be one useful source of publicity for an action or a campaign, but they will never tell our story for us. They cover celebrities instead of issues, events instead of ideas, and 'factions' instead of social movements A direct action movement will only grow through contacts among people in their own communities, on a day-to-day basis…"[26]

Since underfunded social movements cannot afford to advertise to a large audience, they are dependent upon free publicity from the news media. This media coverage may be the only link between isolated individuals and a movement. But as the quote above makes clear, many activists have come to realize that press-mediated accounts are unlikely to significantly help in the recruitment of new members.

Fourth, media coverage that widens the scope of conflict tends to escalate the cost to authorities of using overtly repressive measures in combating rebellious groups. Extralegal violence on the part of authorities becomes substantially more difficult when carried out under the glare of television cameras and under the observation of reporters from major media outlets.

Fifth, media coverage can sometimes aid in both enhancing the sense of a movement's accomplishments and effectiveness and, by publicizing dissent, can delegitimize an authority's position. At the very least, media coverage of challenging groups can help to combat a hegemonic political climate. Media coverage can help establish an issue as a "controversial" one. It can legitimize the positions of some movement organizations, and certify movement spokespeople as "experts". Such legitimization can be a boost to the sense of efficacy felt by movement participants. This last point is well-known to movement fundraisers who often use media clippings as "proof" of an organization's significance.

Ultimately, activists cannot afford to ignore the mainstream media. Most organized political activity includes some relationship, or attempted relationship, with the media. For most activists media contact occurs on a local or regional level, not on the national media stage. Many of the same dynamics that we have described on the national level, though, also operate on the local level—albeit in less rigid form. Activists are likely to have more success gaining access to mainstream local media, particularly if they focus strategic thinking and organizational resources on media work.

But while activists should not ignore the mainstream media, neither should they be preoccupied by it. The reality is that regular access to mainstream media, especially at the national level, is not likely to be granted to voices of dissent. In addition, gaining access to mainstream media will likely be a mixed bag. Rather it will present activists with new challenges. As a result there has sometimes developed a division between social movement activists who make mainstream media the focus of their work and those activists who work in the alternative media. While the differences between these two positions often appear substantial, from a strategic standpoint such divisions are unnecessary and, more important, overlook the important complementary work done by mainstream media activists and alternative media activists.

Media Politics: Mainstream *and* Alternative

We would like to make the case for the importance of addressing mainstream media while at the same time supporting alternative media. Indeed, this volume represents a concrete example of the intermingling of the two areas: studies of mainstream media published by an independent press.

Those activists who work on issues relating to the mainstream media are primarily concerned with critiquing the media and trying to diversify the coverage found there. The sheer pervasiveness of this media makes paying attention to it worthwhile. Given the impact of concentrated corporate ownership of the media and the consequences associated with a largely for-profit news media, little is likely to fundamentally change until ownership of at least some media becomes truly public. But the more immediate goal of media activists is to get the mainstream media to do a better job, that is, to diversify their coverage and to include perspectives and voices that they usually leave out.

However, it would be naive to think that mainstream media are going to unlock the gates and give access to those voices it has always excluded. Our studies and, more importantly, the work of many media activists have done little to significantly change the mainstream media.

This point was driven home by a recent incident. A few months after our study took PBS to task for airing so many business programs while ignoring the economic concerns of working people, PBS announced its newest economic program: *Bloomberg Business News.* One newspaper advertisement, which featured four separate corporate logos, heralded the new program under the headline "In-depth Reporting of Business News that Matters to Professionals."[27] The fact that such reporting may not matter to anyone else seems of little concern to public television.

The incident was symbolic of the fact that analysis, critique, and activism aimed at mainstream media often seems to have little, if any, real impact on changing the media. So the question arises, why do it?

We think there are sound reasons to continue monitoring mainstream media and producing critiques of their performance. First, for people who may not have yet thought critically about the media, such analyses can be food for thought. Especially when reported on in the widely accessible mainstream media, critiques and analyses of the news media can potentially spark people to think more critically about what they are seeing or reading. The mainstream media play a major role in teaching citizens about their community and their world. The engaging technology and easy accessibility of television, especially, makes it the primary source of information for most Americans. One goal of those concerned with the media, therefore, ought to be educating people about how media institutions work and what their limitations are. Understanding how news is gathered, who pays for it, how sources are tapped, and so on can help people become better informed consumers of media information. The point is not to turn off mainstream media, but instead to watch or read news with a critical eye.

Avoiding corporate media, turning off your TV set, and so on may be a fine personal lifestyle choice, but it doesn't help in productively addressing the millions of Americans who will continue to turn to the mainstream media for information. There is a wide variety of resources, including a growing body of literature that critically examines media and several progressive media watch groups that can help to make media consumers better informed about the news that they watch.[28] If activists want to build a more vibrant democracy, one that encourages citizen participation, this kind of "media literacy" work is an area that presents great opportunities.

We suspect that sometimes activists underestimate the level of skepticism that the general public holds towards what they see or read in the media. People are not simply being "duped" by mainstream media products. Instead, they use information culled from media accounts as one ingredient in a mix that also includes knowledge derived from personal experience and the experience of acquaintances. Watching and reading mainstream media—if done with a critical eye—can be quite useful.

Second, research and activism aimed at the news media can help document the impressions of those who already are aware of the shortcomings of mainstream media. The goal here is to provide those already-critical thinkers with evidence and perhaps better ground their critique of the role of media. Moreover, activism that targets mainstream media institutions, even when it does not produce substantial change, can serve to mobilize new activists into broader progressive political work.

Third, while the national media are formidable corporate fortresses whose preoccupation with national "players" precludes most voices of dissent, the local media may be a different story. It is unnecessary defeatism to believe that all media are simply, completely, and unfailingly mouthpieces for those in power. It is giving too much credit to those who support the status quo to believe that they can always control media coverage to their advantage. The occasions when coverage breaks the mold of media-as-usual may be rare, but they are important. Local media can, on occasion, be a useful place to educate about injustice and spotlight change efforts. In the wake of the Gulf war, for example, activists in such cities as San Francisco, Boston, Chicago, Austin, Hartford, and Chapel Hill developed organizations dedicated to local media activism. In several cases, the groups found that the local public television and public radio stations were the most permeable targets. Three years after the

Gulf war, several local media activist groups continue to work with other progressive activists to pressure prominent local media outlets.

Activists know the usefulness, for example, of cultivating working relationships with individual journalists who are willing to seriously consider dissenting points of view. Such journalists are still subject to the control of editors or producers, but their awareness of the existence of alternative views on particular issues can contribute to a broader range of opinion being included in mainstream coverage.

However, positive work can only go so far in relation to the mainstream media. That is why alternative media, that are independent of corporate control, are crucial. It would be difficult to overestimate the importance of such alternative media. Because of the nature of the industry, the mainstream media simply cannot be relied upon to fully communicate alternative views. Only independent, alternative media outlets are able to provide an adequate format to accommodate a full discussion of issues.

Among the many benefits of alternative media is the capability to be on the cutting edge of social and political issues since they are often directly tied into communities promoting social change. Alternative media are also able to nurture authors and artists who otherwise would not find an outlet for their work. While facing extremely limited budget constraints, alternative media outlets can offer more opportunity for in-depth analysis of issues with significant context and historical background provided.

Ideally, then, we see activists whose emphasis is mainstream media complementing the work of alternative media activists, and vice versa. Since the mainstream media are going to remain hostile to challenging ideas, those ideas are likely to be developed and articulated in alternative media sources. Since the majority of Americans will continue to receive their information from the mainstream media, it is important that activists continue to monitor, try to understand, and critique news content. In any case, alternative publications generally present the most insightful criticism of mainstream media and activists focusing on mainstream media, by arguing for more diverse news, often help to make alternative publications more visible to a broader audience.

The Limitations of Mainstream Media Access

Working to change mainstream media has its advantages, as we have pointed out. However, there are also a number of problems that face activists who are trying to improve the mainstream media.

First, is the issue of inadequate resources. Especially on the state and national level, trying to influence mainstream media requires the marshalling of resources that are beyond the reach of most progressive groups. Monitoring and analyzing media products can be a monotonous and time-consuming process that is unlikely to be high on the list of priorities for already over-extended activists. Given limited success in actually changing media coverage, scarce resources may be directed elsewhere.

Second, a concern with mainstream media may confuse the means with the goals. Gaining access to mainstream media is a means to an end. In her sophisticated analysis of media strategies for grassroots organizing, Charlotte Ryan notes that those who engage in political organizing approach the mainstream media for two reasons. First, they want to make the news a "contested terrain." She writes, "The news is an opportunity for challengers, at a minimum, to point out that the establishment view is not the only or 'natural' way to look at a problem and, at best, to present an alternative." The second goal organizers have is "to use media as a vehicle for mobilizing support."[29]

The problem is that too often activists begin to see media coverage as an end in itself. At its worst a deadly dynamic develops. Activists recognize that, because they carry little clout in the debates, the media generally ignore them so they resort to attention-grabbing actions to generate media coverage. Such dramatic actions can backfire in making activists appear as unreasonable "fringe" elements, while those in power can respond without resorting to such gimmicks. The point is not just to generate media coverage, but it is to do so on terms that are favorable to your change efforts.[30]

The media can be useful in promoting the message of a social movement that has a solid and active constituency. But such coverage comes after people have been organized, not the other way around. Too often activists seek media coverage without having done the more fundamental groundwork of political organizing. This means their strategies tend to be geared towards getting covered in the media rather than necessarily communicating an effective message or mobilizing others to join in an effort.

Third, mainstream media formats are usually quite brief. The seven-second soundbite, for example, is a staple of television news. This presents special problem for progressives who are trying to challenge conventional wisdom. Because of the fast-pace and short story-format in the news media, someone presenting a challenging view is usually not given the time or space to cite evidence for these views. Conventional platitudes require no evidence and can be fit into mainstream media formats. Challenging views cannot. As a result, those who express dissident views—but who don't have the time or space to supply evidence or elaborate—are likely to appear unreasonable to someone previously unfamiliar with their arguments.[31]

The Limitations of Alternative Media

A strategy exclusively focused on alternative media also presents some major shortcomings. Most importantly, alternative media are capable of reaching only a limited audience—usually of those already sympathetic to an issue. Despite much fanfare about the proliferation of media technologies and the possibilities for new communication avenues that side-step major corporate control, the major media outlets which continue to wield the most influence continue to be controlled by a relatively small group of corporate conglomerates. The reality is that because of the globalization of media and the ever-increasing cost of producing top-quality, competitive media-products, it is more difficult—not less—for alternative media to have an impact on political and social debates.

The high cost of television production, for example, has meant that progressive alternative programming has been limited in quality and reach. Local public access programs can sometimes be useful in addressing overlooked issues and perspectives, but clearly such programming is quite limited in audience and impact.

Second, alternative media simply do not have the resources to cover the many issues that may be of interest to people. There are no progressive publications that can match the network of reporters and resources regularly called upon by the mainstream press. Thus, given the alternative press' reliance on writers who are able and willing to contribute their work for little or no pay, alternative media reporting can be spotty in coverage and uneven in quality.

Most fundamentally, alternative media can help to nurture and sustain social movements, allow new ideas to emerge, and regularly challenge the boundaries set by mainstream media, but they do not have the capability to reach large numbers of citizens. To the extent that progressive activists want to broaden their movement and the circles within which progressive perspectives are circulated, alternative media institutions can only go so far.

If the point of political organizing is to mobilize those who are not already politically active, then it is important to understand how such non-participants learn about the issues. Relying exclusively on alternative media for information can prevent activists from understanding how others learn about policy debates and contemporary issues.

The Future of Media "Activism"
Ours is, in part, a cautionary tale, eschewing simple solutions to complex media issues. We end here with a few more words of caution for those interested in addressing the area of news media.

If activists are to be consistent in their demands for a more diverse and inclusive media they must refrain from simply mimicking calls from the right. That is, as we have tried to show, it does no good to approach the media with the simple claim of "bias." That's because claims of bias too often hide implicit claims to understanding Truth that, in turn, limit, rather than promote, debate and discussion. Saying the media "got it wrong" on a story suggests that there is a clear correct position to be upheld. Of course, factual errors do occur in reporting and they need to be pointed out and corrected. But most reality is rarely that simple and media coverage ought to be incorporating different interpretations of this complex reality.

We are troubled, too, by a media activism that fatalistically focuses exclusively on the "evils" of mainstream media. It is crucially important to understand the propagandistic uses to which the media are directed. However, the importance of even the occasional presence of dissenting voices should not be discounted. The walls of the corporate media fortresses are not without their fissures. While admittedly a difficult struggle, criticism of mainstream media must be coupled with a call to open the gates of such media to provide for more diverse access and ultimately for public ownership of some media outlets. Linking criticism with organizing for change is not naive, it is necessary. The long-term goal of media activism is the restucturing of the media so that news promotes diverse discussion and debate. A more democratic media system will require a fundamentally different ownership structure, one that is neither highly concentrated in the hands of a small number of private interests nor shaped by homogenizing pressures associated with a for-profit orientation and a reliance on major advertisers.

Currently, the media limit political debate by the narrow range of stories they address and, even more importantly, by the limited range of voices and perspectives regularly featured as part of their coverage. As long as commentary and analysis of public affairs is provided by a narrow range of individuals representing powerful corporate and government interests, inclusive democratic debate that truly reflects the diversity of our society will not exist. Dissent and diversity will not be found, as long as access to the mainstream media is granted by invitation only.

Notes

Introduction

1   "Are You on the *Nightline* Guest List?" *Extra!*. Vol. 2, No. 4, January/February 1989; "All The Usual Suspects: *MacNeil/Lehrer* and *Nightline*." *Extra!*. Vol. 3, No. 4, Special Issue, 1990; "Public Television & the Missing Public." *Extra!*. Vol. 6, No. 6, September/October 1993. A different version of the *Nightline* study appeared as "The Chosen Few: *Nightline* and the Politics of Public Affairs Television." *Critical Sociology*, 18 (1): 19-34.

2   See, for example, "Ted Koppel's Edge." *New York Times Magazine*, Marshall Blonsky, August 14, 1988; "America's Q&A Man." *Newsweek* June 15, 1987; "The Man Who Wouldn't Be King." *Esquire*, January, 1984.

3   David Croteau, William Hoynes, and Kevin M. Carragee. "Public Television 'Prime Time': Public Affairs Programming, Political Diversity, and the Conservative Critique of Public Television." Unpublished Report, August, 1993.

Chapter 1

1   Jann Wenner and William Greider, "The Rolling Stone Interview: President Clinton." *Rolling Stone*, December 9, 1993.

2   *Nightline*'s debate between Will and Moyers was broadcast on May 12, 1992. Others quoted in the background piece were conservative activist Brent Bozell, U.S. Senators Jesse Helms and Bob Dole, and the Heritage Foundation's Laurence Jarvik, along with then-PBS President Bruce Christensen and Producer Ken Burns. See also Bill Carter, "Conservatives Call for PBS to Go Private or Go Dark." *New York Times*. April 30, 1992, p. 1. The same pattern is visible here. Jarvik, Dole, and Robert Lichter provide the conservative critique of PBS and Christensen and

BIll Moyers defend PBS.

3 See for example, Brent L. Bozel III and Brent A. Baker, *And That's the Way It Isn't: A Reference Guide to Media Bias* (Alexandria, VA: Media Research Center, 1991); David Horowitz, "The Politics of Public Television." *Commentary*, 92: 25-32; Laurence Jarvik, "Making Public Television Public." The Heritage Foundation. January 18, 1992; S. Robert Lichter, Daniel Amundson, and Linda Lichter. "Balance and Diversity in PBS Documentaries." Center for Media and Public Affairs. March, 1992; S. Robert Lichter, et. al., *The Media Elite: America's New Power Brokers* (Mamaroneck, NY: Hastings, 1990).

4 John Stuart Mill, *On Liberty*. (New York: Viking, 1982).

5 Quoted in Mark Hertsgaard, *On Bended Knee* (New York: Schocken Books, 1988), p. 62.

6 Robert Woodward and Carl Bernstein, *All the President's Men*. (New York: Simon & Schuster, 1974).

7 Project Censored at Sonoma State University annually compiles and publishes a list of the top ten stories neglected by the mainstream media. See, for example, "The top censored stories of 1993." *Utne Reader*, No. 63, May/June, 1994, pp. 42-47.

8 For discussion of the journalist-source relationship, see Leon V. Sigal, *Reporters and Officials: The Organization and Politics of Newsmaking* (Lexington, MA: Heath, 1973); and Herbert Gans, *Deciding What's News* (New York: Vintage, 1979).

9 For a thoughtful discussion of the political implications of "objective" reporting, see W. Lance Bennett. *News: The Politics of Illusion*, second edition. (White Plains, NY: Longman, 1988).

10 For a discussion of news beats, see Gaye Tuchman, *Making News* (New York: The Free Press, 1978).

11 Quoted from ABC's *Nightline*, September 27, 1989. Deaver's news management skills are also explored in Mark Hertsgaard, *On Bended Knee* (New York: Schocken Books, 1988).

12 Quoted from ABC's *Nightline*, September 27, 1989.

13 See Robert Parry and Peter Kornbluh, "Iran-Contra's Untold Story." *Foreign Policy*, Fall 1988.

14 Stephen Kurkjian, "Restraining the media at the CIA." *Boston Globe*, August 22, 1989.

15 Walter Robinson, "Journalists constrained by Pentagon." *Boston Globe*. December 25, 1989, p. 3.

16 See John MacArthur, *Second Front: Censorship & Propaganda in the Gulf War* (New York: Hill & Wang, 1992) and Douglas Kellner, *The Persian Gulf TV War* (Boulder, CO: Westview, 1992), for a thorough analysis of media coverage and military-media relations during the Gulf War. For an examination of military restrictions on the media during the invasions of Grenada and Panama, as well as the Gulf War, see Jacqueline Sharkey, *Under Fire* (Washington, DC: The Center for Public Integrity, 1991).

17 For a thoughtful analysis of the potential for media to make politics more public, see Jeffrey B. Abramson, F. Christopher Arterton, and Gary R. Orren, *The Electronic Commonwealth* (New York: Basic Books, 1988).

18 Doug Underwood, *When MBA's Rule the Newsroom* (New York: Columbia University Press, 1993), p. xii.

19 See Boorstein's discussion of pseudo-events. Daniel Boorstein, *The Image* (New York: Atheneum, 1962).

20 See John Anthony Maltese, *Spin Control: The White House Office of Communications and the Management of Presidential News*, second edition (Chapel Hill: University of North Carolina Press, 1994) for a thorough discussion of presidential news management.

21 For further analysis of the contemporary news media, see Douglas Kellner, *Television and the Crisis of Democracy* (Boulder, CO: Westview, 1990); Martin Lee and Norman Solomon, *Unreliable Sources* (New York: Lyle Stuart, 1989); and W. Lance Bennett, *News: The Politics of Illusion* (White Plains, NY: Longman, 1990).

22 Ben Bagdikian, *The Media Monopoly*, fourth edition (Boston: Beacon Press, 1992).

23 Quoted in B. Owen, *Economics and Freedom of Expression* (Cambridge, MA: Ballinger, 1975), p. 1.

24 For a more thorough discussion of corporate funding and the relationship between funding and programming within public television, see William Hoynes, *Public Television for Sale* (Boulder, CO: Westview Press, 1994).

25 Accuracy in Media, and its chairman Reed Irvine, have made the most vociferous charges of this nature. See Walter Schneir and Miriam Schneir, "The Right's Attack on the Press." *The Nation*, March 30, 1985, pp. 361-367.

26 Of course, this does not preclude criticism of the media for issues of straightforward accuracy. As the corrections box in most newspapers makes clear, there *are* some fundamental facts about which reasonable people can agree—and about which journalists are sometimes wrong. But the inaccurate reporting of, say, the name of a person's employer or the date of an event, is not the sort of issue that usually generates the political debates in which we are interested here.

27 James L. Tyson, *Target America: The Influence of Communist Propaganda on U.S. Media* (Chicago: Regnery Gateway, 1981), pp. 223-224.

28 See Sharon Bernstein, "PBS Vows to Take Offensive Against Critics." *Los Angeles Times*, June 25, 1992, and Laurie Oullette, "Right Wing vs. Public TV." *MediaCulture Review*, December, 1991.

29 Frederic M. Biddle, "Flap erupts as PBS refuses to fund 'More Tales of the City.'" *Boston Globe*, April 13, 1994, p. 76. Andrew Kopkind. "Chilling Tales." *The Nation*, May 2, 1994.

30 The distinction, though, is not always simple. There are some progressives who argue for the censoring of some material, for example, pornography and various sorts of hate speech. We generally find such positions troubling and counter to an over-all orientation of free and diverse speech.

31 Data on gender is cited in Martin Lee and Norman Solomon, *Unreliable Sources* (New York: Lyle Stuart, 1989).

32 M. Goldin, "Father time: Who's on the op-ed page?" *Mother Jones*, January 1990, p. 51.

33 Barbara Reynolds, "For Media Decision-Makers, Urban Problems Are Old News." *Extra!*, July/August, 1992, p. 12.

34 Cited in Alicia C. Shepard, "High Anxiety." *American Journalism Review*, November, 1993, pp. 19-24.

Chapter 2

1 For a broader discussion of these issues, see James Davison Hunter, *Culture Wars: The Struggle to Define America* (New York: Basic Books, 1991).

2 Quoted from *Race Against Prime Time*, California Newsreel.

3 Quoted from *The Eleventh Hour*. May 21, 1990.

4   Quoted in *Extra!*, 4:3, May 1991.

5   Thanks to Greg Bates for highlighting this aspect of our argument.

6   See Shanto Iyengar and Donald R. Kinder, *News That Matters: Television and American Opinion* (Chicago: University of Chicago Press, 1987), for a useful discussion of agenda setting.

7   Brian McGrory, "Relationship of crime news, fear is debated." *Boston Globe*, May 4, 1994, pp. 1, 4.

8   Quoted from *The Eleventh Hour*. May 21, 1990.

9   Jay Rosen, "Who Won the Week? The Political Press and the Evacuation of Meaning." *Tikkun*, 8:4, p. 9.

10   For analysis of the associates of prominent thinktanks that appear regularly on the evening news, see Lawrence Storey, *The News Shapers* (New York: Praeger, 1992). For a more general discussion of the role of Washington "pundits" in the media see Eric Alterman, *Sound & Fury* (New York: HarperPerennial, 1992).

Chapter 3

1   See, for example, W. Lance Bennett, *News: The Politics of Illusion* (White Plains, NY: Longman, 1990); Edward Jay Epstein, *News From Nowhere* (New York: Vintage, 1973); Herbert Gans, *Deciding What's News* (New York: Vintage, 1979); Peter Golding and Philip Elliot, *Making the News* (London: Longmans, 1979); Edward S. Herman and Noam Chomsky, *Manufacturing Consent* (New York: Pantheon, 1988); Mark Hertsgaard, *On Bended Knee* (New York: Schocken Books, 1988); Martin Lee and Norman Solomon, *Unreliable Sources* (New York: Lyle Stuart, 1989); Michael Schudson, *Discovering the News* (New York: Basic Books, 1978); Leon V. Sigal, *Reporters and Officials: The Organization and Politics of Newsmaking* (Lexington, MA: Heath, 1973); Gaye Tuchman, *Making News* (New York: The Free Press, 1978); Doug Underwood, *When MBA's Rule the Newsroom* (New York: Columbia University Press, 1993).

2   See, for example, Peter Golding and Philip Elliot, *Making the News* (London: Longmans, 1979); Herbert Gans, *Deciding What's News* (New York: Vintage, 1979); Edward S. Herman

and Noam Chomsky, *Manufacturing Consent* (New York: Pantheon, 1988).

3 *Life*, October 1988.

4 For discussion of media "frames," see William A. Gamson, *Talking Politics* (New York: Cambridge University Press, 1992); Charlotte Ryan, *Prime Time Activism* (Boston: South End Press, 1991); and Todd Gitlin, *The Whole World is Watching* (Berkeley: University of California Press, 1980).

5 *Boston Globe Magazine*, November 6, 1988.

6 Herbert Gans, *Deciding What's News* (New York: Vintage, 1979), pp. 304-335.

7 George Will is a special case, given his close relationship to the Reagan White House and his unique position at ABC News as an opinion commentator, not just a correspondent or analyst. With twelve appearances, Will's views were heard as frequently as Jerry Falwell and Elliott Abrams. But since he is on the ABC News staff, we do not list him as an invited guest.

8 Seymour Hersh, *The Price of Power: Kissinger in the Nixon White House* (New York: Summit Books, 1983).

9 Jesse Jackson, as presidential candidate and leader of the Rainbow Coalition, is more than a spokesperson for African-Americans; he is also a spokesperson for many public interest constituencies. We, therefore, have classified Jackson as a public interest leader, rather than a racial/ethnic leader, for the purposes of this study.

10 We calculate the early appearance rate by dividing the number of appearances before the first commercial break by the total number of appearances.

11 Edward Herman, *The Real Terror Network* (Boston: South End Press, 1982).

12 While "Viewpoint" programs are produced by Nightline's staff, decisions about issues and guests involve ABC News executives who do not normally play a direct role in *Nightline*'s programming.

13 Most U.S. mass media cover business extensively and largely ignore labor. Virtually every daily newspaper, for example, has a business section; we know of none that has a regular section on labor news.

14 On a program about South Africa pitting a State Department spokesperson against U.S. anti-apartheid leader and divestment

proponent Randall Robinson (8/26/86), Koppel discounted the utility of U.S. corporate disengagement by suggesting that U.S. corporations "are a force for positive social change." His statement echoed the Reagan policy of constructive engagement. In programs featuring Nicaragua's Alejandro Bendana (e.g., 5/14/87 and 10/7/87), Koppel questioned Bendana—in conformity with U.S. premises—about Nicaragua's "wonderful propaganda campaign," its plans "to turn back all the democratic advances," and its propensity for offering "rhetoric" instead of "serious proposals."

15 Gaye Tuchman, "Introduction" in *The TV Establishment* (Englewood Cliffs, NJ: Prentice-Hall, 1974.

16 Prior to launching his late-1980's nightly interview program, Moyers told the *New York Times* that his program would "promote the conversation of democracy" by "bringing to television voices that do not normally get heard, left and right, conservative and liberal, socialists and libertarians." Moyers' attitude is commendable, but unfortunately very rare in television.

17 *Boston Globe*, October 31, 1988.

18 Peace movement spokesperson, Dr. Benjamin Spock, did appear recently on *Nightline*...to discuss circumcision (8/4/88). When Theresa and Blase Bonpane, leading critics of U.S. policy in Central America, got their chance on *Nightline*, it was to discuss "Priests and Celibacy" (3/29/83).

Chapter 4

1 Charlayne Hunter-Gault, "MacNeil/Lehrer, TV's Finest Hour." V*ogue*, January, 1984, p. 255.

2 Carnegie Commission on Educational Television, *Public Television: A Program for Action* (New York: Bantam, 1967).

3 Robert MacNeil, *The People Machine: The Influence of Television on American Politics* (New York: Harper & Row, 1968).

4 Quoted in James Traub, "That (too long?) one-hour news show." *Columbia Journalism Review*, January/February 1985, p. 42.

5 James Traub, "That (too long?) one-hour news show." *Columbia Journalism Review*, January/February 1985, p. 41.

6 Jerome L. Himmelstein, *To the Right: The Transformation of American Conservatism* (Berkeley: University of California

Press: 1990).

7   Race was identifiable for 90 percent of guests.

8   Quoted in Mark Hertsgaard, "Covering the World: Ignoring the Earth." *Rolling Stone*, November 16, 1989, p. 49.

9   See "Human Rights and the Media," *Extra!*, Summer 1989.

10 James Traub, "That (too long?) one-hour news show." *Columbia Journalism Review*, January/February 1985, p. 42.

11 Quoted in Robert Karl Manoff, "Quick-Fix News: MacNeil/Lehrer plays it safe." *The Progressive*, July, 1987, p. 15.

12 Judith Michaelson, "Koppel, Producer Challenge Report, Say Show Is a News Program, Not Equal-Access Forum." *Los Angeles Times*, February 6, 1989, part VI, p. 12.

Chapter 5

1   Carnegie Commission on Educational Television, *Public Television: A Program for Action* (New York: Bantam, 1967).

2   See David M. Stone, *Nixon and the Politics of Public Television* (New York: Garland Publishing, 1985).

3   See "Facts About PBS, " distributed by PBS; Lewis Lapham, "Adieu, Big Bird: On the Terminal Irrelevance of Public Television." *Harper's* December, 1993; and William Hoynes, *Public Television for Sale* (Boulder, CO: Westview Press, 1994).

4   Laurence Jarvik. "Making Public Television Public." (Washington, DC: The Heritage Foundation, 1992).

5   Data on cable television is from "National Audience Report," Winter Quarter 1992, from PBS Research, which is based on data from the Nielsen Television Index.

6   David Horowitz, "The Politics of Public Television." *Commentary*, 1991, 92: 25-32.

7   Quoted in Patti Hartigan, "Targeting PBS," *Boston Globe*, March 4, 1992.

8   Quoted in Bill Carter, "Conservatives Call for PBS to Go Private or Go Dark." *New York Times*, April 30, 1992.

9   Quoted in D. Benz, "In the Life: PBS Keeps Its Distance From Gay Programming." *Extra!*, 1993, 6: 4, p. 17.

10 McCain and Helms quoted in Martin Tolchin, "Public Broadcasting Bill is Sidelined." *New York Times*, March 5, 1992, p. A14.

11 Public Telecommunications Act of 1992. [Public Law 102-356]

12 S. R. Lichter, D. Amundson, and L. S. Lichter. "Balance and Diversity in PBS Documentaries." (Washington, DC: Center for Media and Public Affairs, 1992). For a persuasive critique of this study, see Jim Naureckas, "Study of Bias or Biased Study?: The Lichter Method and the Attack on PBS Documentaries." FAIR Research Memo, May 14, 1992.

13 The Winter, 1992 "National Audience Report," produced by PBS Research, indicates that the prime-time rating was 2.3, compared to a daytime rating of 1.1. One rating point in 1992 equaled 921,000 households.

14 We did not include science and technology nor nature programs in public affairs because, while some of these programs do feature political content, as a whole they do not consistently address policy debates.

15 Though we coded for race, the percentage of sources for whom race was unidentifiable made it impossible to meaningfully use this data.

16 All of the live "general public" sources, six Canadian students, appeared on one edition of Firing Line.

17 See Charlotte Ryan, "A Study of National Public Radio." Extra!, 1993, 6: 3, pp. 18-21, 26.

18 Daniel Hallin, "Cartography, Community, and the Cold War." in R.K. Manoff and M. Schudson, eds. Reading the News (New York: Pantheon, 1986).

19 Efforts to place this type of program on the public television lineup have met with a decidedly chilly reception from PBS. Most recently, We Do The Work, a monthly program focusing on the lives of working people (which airs on a small number of public television stations but is not distributed by PBS), has faced these charges.

Chapter 6

1 Howard Rosenberg, "Same Faces in Political Crowd (White Males), Same Viewpoints Recycled on Issues of the Day." Los Angeles Times, February 6, 1989.

2 Judith Michaelson, "'Nightline' attacked for conservatism." Los Angeles Times, February 7, 1989.

3 Judith Michaelson, "Koppel, Producer Challenge Report, Say Show Is a News Program, Not Equal-Access Forum." Los

Angeles Times, February 6, 1989.

4   Jeremy Gerard, "TV Notes: 'Nightline criticized by a monitoring group." *New York Times*, February 6, 1989.

5   Marc Gunther, "'MacNeil/Lehrer' show is narrow-minded, study says." *Detroit Free Press*, May 21, 1990.

6   There is reason to believe that this was helpful in CISPES broader organizing strategy. CISPES referred to the *Nightline* appearance in their subsequent fundraising appeals.

7   Joseph Kahn, "Nightline guest list called biased." *Boston Globe*, February 6, 1989.

8   Quoted from *The Eleventh Hour*. May 21, 1990.

9   K.E.B., "Can we hear more from the Average Joe? —and Josie?" *Current*, September 6, 1993.

10 John Horn, "Study finds 'Nightline' favors male conservatives." *Ann Arbor News*, February 6, 1989.

11 Judith Michaelson, "Koppel, Producer Challenge Report, Say Show Is a News Program, Not Equal-Access Forum." *Los Angeles Times*, February 6, 1989.

12 Joseph Kahn, "Nightline guest list called biased." *Boston Globe*, February 6, 1989.

13 Judith Michaelson, "Koppel, Producer Challenge Report, Say Show Is a News Program, Not Equal-Access Forum." *Los Angeles Times*, February 6, 1989.

14 Walter Goodman, "Watchdog Group Criticizes 2 News Programs." *New York Times*, May 28, 1990.

15 Laura Fraser, "Who's on the 'Nightline' guest list." *San Francisco Bay Guardian*, February 15, 1989.

16 Laura Fraser, "Who's on the 'Nightline' guest list." *San Francisco Bay Guardian*, February 15, 1989.

17 John Horn, "Study finds 'Nightline' favors male conservatives." *Ann Arbor News*, February 6, 1989.

18 John Carman, "Liberal Group Calls 'Nightline' Biased." *San Francisco Chronicle*, February 6, 1989.

19 "Talking heads and warm feet." *The Berkshire Eagle*, February 12, 1989.

20 Clarence Page, "Conservatives find roost on the 'Nightline.'" *Cleveland Plain Dealer*, February 15, 1989.

21 Howard Rosenberg, "Same Faces in Political Crowd (White Males), Same Viewpoints Recycled on Issues of the Day." *Los Angeles Times*, February 6, 1989.

22 Tracey Wong Briggs, "PBS 'bias' missing in programs." *USA Today*, August 23, 1993.

23 Walter Goodman, "Watchdog Group Criticizes 2 News Programs," *New York Times*, May 28, 1990.

24 For a discussion of working class skepticism towards politicians and the electoral process see chapter 4 of David Croteau, *Politics and the Class Divide: Working People and the Middle Class Left* (Philadelphia: Temple University Press, 1994).

25 For a discussion of the political economy of new media technologies, see W. Russell Neuman, *The Future of the Mass Audience* (New York: Cambridge University Press, 1991).

26 Coalition for Direct Action at Seabrook. *It Won't Be Built: Seabrook Occupation/Blockade Handbook*, 1980.

27 Advertisement in *Boston Globe*, March 30, 1994, p. 45.

28 For a list of alternative media, readings about media, and media analysis groups, see the appendices to Martin Lee and Norman Solomon, *Unreliable Sources* (New York: Lyle Stuart, 1989).

29 Charlotte Ryan, *Prime Time Activism.* (Boston: South End Press, 1991), p. 4.

30 See Todd Gitlin, *The Whole World is Watching* (Berkeley: University of California Press, 1980), for a comprehensive analysis of the relationship between media and the New Left.

31 The consequence of the media's time/space limitation for progressives was brought to our attention by Noam Chomsky in personal correspondence (May 28, 1989) from which we paraphrase here.

Index

Index

Index

Index

Index

Index